Presented To:

Hannah Marie Porter

Date:

Christmas, 2004

TO THE MOST
SPECIAL LITTLE
GIRL IN THE
WORLD.
    LOVE,
Daddy

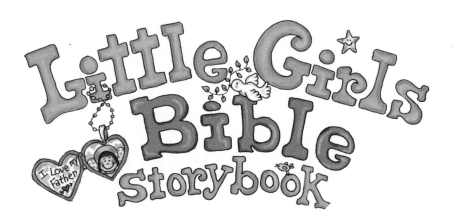

Little Girls Bible Storybook

Fathers And Daughters

Text copyright © 2000 by Carolyn Larsen
Illustrations copyright © 2000 by Caron Turk

New Kids Media™ is published by Baker Book House
Company, Grand Rapids, Michigan.

Third printing, July 2001

Printed in the United States of America

ISBN 0-8010-4469-3

Scripture quotations are taken from the Holy Bible, New
Living Translation, copyright © 1996. Used by permission of
Tyndale House Publishers, Inc., Wheaton, Illinois 60189. All
rights reserved.

For current information about all releases from Baker Book
House, visit our web site:
                    http://www.bakerbooks.com

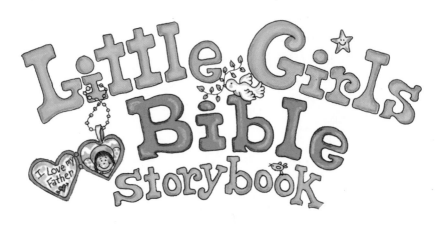

Little Girls Bible Storybook

 Fathers  Daughters

Carolyn Larsen

Illustrated by Caron Turk

NEW KiDs MEDiA

BAKER
A DIVISION OF
Baker Book House Co

Contents

Dear Dads,

The relationship a little girl has with her dad is so important. A good relationship helps establish a good self-image and self-confidence. Most little girls think their dads can do absolutely anything. Dad has a unique ability to teach his daughter the truths of the Bible and how to apply Scripture to life.

The Little Girls Bible Storybook for Fathers and Daughters provides an opportunity to look at well-loved Bible stories through the eyes and hearts of the Bible characters who lived them. We don't really know how these people felt about the experiences they lived through. But, they were people like we are, so we can imagine how they felt. By thinking about how these people may have felt, we can learn lessons of how to apply Scripture to our lives and how to make God real in every aspect of life.

Caron Turk has once again hidden a little angel in each illustration. I know that you and your little girl will have fun looking for this little angel. Hopefully, you'll be able to discuss the Bible story as you do your angel search. Caron and I pray that this book will provide hours of "together time" and entertainment with a purpose for you and your daughter. We pray that you will grow closer together and that both you and your daughter will go deeper in your relationship with the Lord through reading and talking about this book.

God bless,

Carolyn Larsen

Someone Like Me

Plink, plink, plink, splash! Adam absentmindedly skipped rocks across a lake filled with water so blue that it almost hurt his eyes. He didn't even seem to notice the animals playing around him. Tiring of the rock-skipping game, Adam leaned back against a tree and heaved a big sigh.

"What's the matter, Son? You don't seem very happy," the Father asked gently.

"I'm sorry, Father. I don't know what's wrong. Maybe I'm a little, ummmmm, lonely," Adam didn't mean to be disrespectful. After all, God had given him a beautiful garden to live in and lots of different kinds of animals to play with.

"I know what's wrong," the Father said, still very gently. "You need someone to talk to-someone who is more like you than any of the animals are."

"Yeah! I think you're right," Adam jumped to his feet in excitement. "But, there isn't anyone here like me. So what do we do?"

"Why don't you take a nap while I work on this?" God seemed to be smiling as he spoke.

Carefully, so as not to disturb Adam's sleep, God gently tugged a rib from Adam's side and used it to make a new person. She was sort of like Adam, but not exactly. "Welcome to earth, Eve. You will be Adam's wife," God was extra gentle now. Eve looked around at the beautiful flowers and rivers. She saw soft bunnies and fuzzy squirrels playing in the grass. She knew that she would be very happy here.

"Adam, wake up," God whispered. Adam opened his eyes and saw a woman with long, curly hair. She smiled shyly at him. "This is Eve," God said. "She will be your wife. I know you will be very happy together. I made you both to be a lot like me. You can think and talk and laugh and cry. I'd like you to take care of things here in the garden."

Adam took Eve's hand. It felt nice. Adam knew that he wouldn't ever be lonely again.

Based on Genesis 1-2

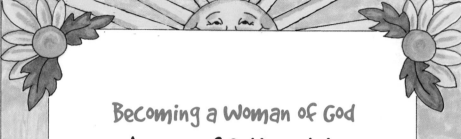

Becoming a Woman of God

A woman of God is made in God's image.

God made people in his image. That means we are a lot like him. It's important for us to remember that all people are made in God's image. When we remember this, we will treat other people with kindness and respect.

It's also important to remember that God made you to be exactly the way he wants you to be. So, be happy with who you are and be thankful for the things you can do!

Dad's Turn

Tell your daughter a story about a skill or ability that God gave you-skill in sports or music, or a love for science or history. Tell her how you have worked to develop that skill or ability.

It's important for your daughter to know how special she is to you. Help her develop a good self-image by pointing out the special things you love about her—her sense of humor, how kind she is, a sports skill or love for music.

A Verse to Remember

So God created people in his own image; God patterned them after himself.

Genesis 1:27

Win or Lose, by What You Choose

"Laaa, daaa laaa, daaa," Eve hummed a happy tune as she pulled a shiny piece of fruit from the tree. Settling down on a warm rock, she thanked the Father for providing everything she and Adam needed, then she took a juicy bite. "Mmm, good!" she thought. She was enjoying it so much that she didn't even notice the snake slithering toward her.

17

And the Lord God planted a garden toward the east, in Eden... and God caused to grow the tree of Knowledge...

"Let'sssss just ssssay I'm a friend"

"Why are you eating that plain old fruit, when you could be having the sweetest, juiciest fruit in the garden?" the snake hissed.

He surprised Eve so she jumped when he spoke. "Who are you? I've never seen you in the garden before."

"Let'sss just sssay I'm a friend," he hissed again. "Want some really good fruit?"

"I've tasted all the fruit here-and it's all good," Eve turned to walk away.

"Actually, there's one fruit you've never tasted," the snake sounded very wise.

"Only from the tree that God told us not to touch," this time Eve did walk away.

"Come on, just taste it. It's good . . . and eating it will make you more like God." The snake dangled the shiny red fruit in Eve's face. It sure looked good.

the serpent was a crafty beast.....

This was a sad day for Adam and Eve

"More like God," Eve thought, "hmmm, that sounds good." She took a bite before she could chicken out. "Wow! This IS good! Adam, try this!" she cried.

Adam recognized the fruit right away. "Eve, what are you doing? God said we would die if we even touched this tree!"

"Do I look dead to you? Try it! It's yummy!" Eve was very convincing and soon Adam was gobbling down the fruit. Right away, though, Adam knew they had done something very, very wrong.

God didn't even try to hide his disappointment. "You have to leave this beautiful garden," he said sadly. "You can't live here anymore."

"I'm sorry we disobeyed you," Adam whispered.

"Me, too," Eve said softly. "The snake made it sound so good. But, I should have remembered how much you love us. I'm so, so sorry."

"I know," God said, "I have to punish you. But that doesn't mean I don't love you—I'll always love you—no matter what."

Based on Genesis 3

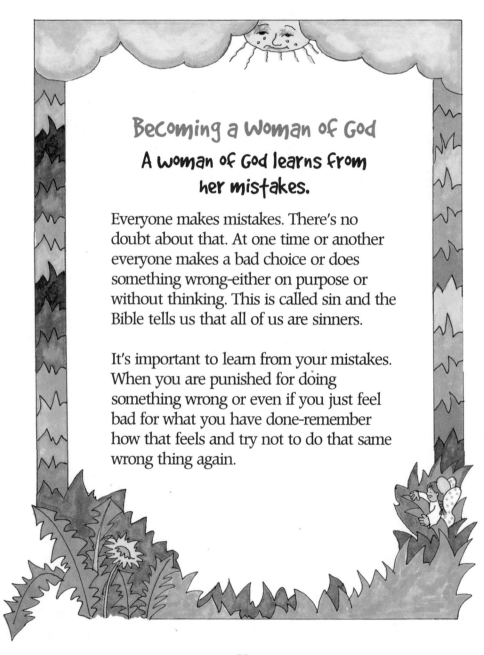

Becoming a Woman of God

A Woman of God learns from her mistakes.

Everyone makes mistakes. There's no doubt about that. At one time or another everyone makes a bad choice or does something wrong-either on purpose or without thinking. This is called sin and the Bible tells us that all of us are sinners.

It's important to learn from your mistakes. When you are punished for doing something wrong or even if you just feel bad for what you have done-remember how that feels and try not to do that same wrong thing again.

Dad's Turn

Can you recall a time in your childhood when you disobeyed your parents? Tell your daughter what you did and what the outcome was. How did you feel after you disobeyed? How did you feel about being punished?

Ask your daughter if she recalls a time when she disobeyed. Does that memory stop her from disobeying in the same way again? Remind your daughter how much you love her and how proud you are of her when she obeys. Remind her that nothing will ever change the love you have for her.

A Verse to Remember

If we confess our sins to him, he is faithful and just to forgive us and to cleanse us from every wrong.

1 John 1:9

Houseboat Safety

Genesis 7-9

"I miss my friends," Noah's wife sighed. "I know God said to build this boat, but . . ."

"I know," Noah interrupted. "If people would just start obeying God again. Then he wouldn't be sending a flood and we wouldn't be building this boat . . . and our friends wouldn't think we're crazy!"

"And, all these animals wouldn't be coming," Mrs. Noah shivered when she saw the snakes and spiders.

Of course, God was right about the flood. As soon as the animals and the Noah family had climbed inside the boat, it started to rain outside. Mrs. Noah missed sunshine and fresh air. But, she kept busy caring for the animals and keeping the boat clean. "It's rained for more than a month," she thought one night. "The whole earth must be flooded by now." It made her sad to think that all her friends had drowned. "Why didn't they just listen to God?" she wondered.

One morning when Mrs. Noah woke up she noticed that
something was different. "Hmm, what could it be?" Suddenly she
knew, "Noah, the rain has stopped!" Just as she said that, the boat
bumped something and dishes tumbled from shelves and tables.

"Ground! We've hit ground!" Noah shouted. He peeked out
and saw that the boat was sitting on the very tip top of a big
mountain. All around them was water.

Day after day Noah checked to see if the flood waters were gone. Finally, one day he called, "I'm opening the door. We can leave the boat!"

"Yahoo!" Mrs. Noah shooed out animals and grabbed a broom. Quickly sweeping the boat clean, she joined Noah on wonderful, dry ground. She grabbed Noah's hand and danced in joy.

The Noah family were the only people left on earth. The first thing they did was thank God for keeping them safe in the great big, sort of smelly, kind of crowded houseboat. Right in the middle of the celebrating, Mrs. Noah noticed colorful arches in the sky, "What is that?" she asked.

"It's a rainbow," God answered. "It's a symbol of my promise to you-I will never send a flood to destroy the whole earth again. So, every time you see a rainbow, remember how very much I love you!"

Based on Genesis 7-9

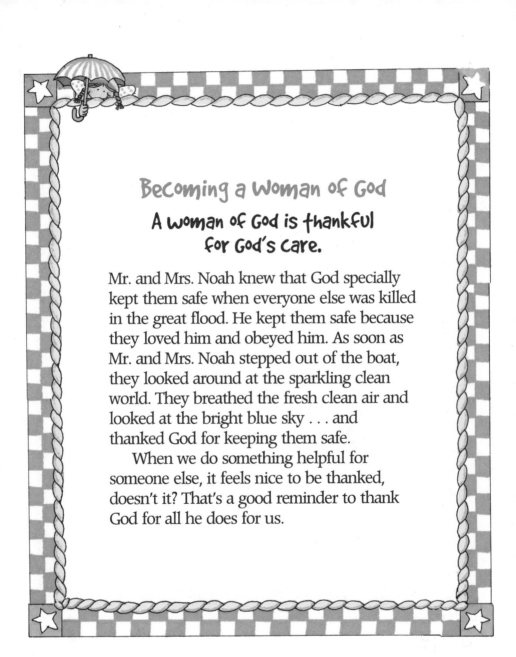

Becoming a Woman of God

A woman of God is thankful for God's care.

Mr. and Mrs. Noah knew that God specially kept them safe when everyone else was killed in the great flood. He kept them safe because they loved him and obeyed him. As soon as Mr. and Mrs. Noah stepped out of the boat, they looked around at the sparkling clean world. They breathed the fresh clean air and looked at the bright blue sky . . . and thanked God for keeping them safe.

When we do something helpful for someone else, it feels nice to be thanked, doesn't it? That's a good reminder to thank God for all he does for us.

Dad's Turn

Tell your daughter about the most memorable rainbow you've ever seen. Where were you? Was it a complete rainbow or perhaps a double one? Why do you remember it?

Talk about some of the ways God takes care of you and your family. Talk about the way he keeps you safe, how he provides a home and food for you and people who love you. Take a few minutes and thank him for all he has given you.

Remind your daughter of a time she expressed thanks for something and how proud you were of her for doing that.

A Verse to Remember

Give thanks to the LORD, for he is good!

1 Chronicles 16:34

L ot sighed and leaned his chair back on two legs. Lot's life was good-he had lots of sheep, cattle and hundreds of men working for him.

Lot's uncle, Abram, was even richer in gold, silver, sheep, cattle and people working for him. Both clans had just set up camp near the Jordan River.

"Hey, get your sheep out of here. We got here first!" Lot's shepherds shouted. They poked at Abram's sheep with their staffs, trying to shove them out of the way. Pretty soon the two groups of men were pushing each other and shouting. The sheep didn't know what to think.

Abram sat outside his tent and listened to the arguing. "This isn't right," he thought, "someone is going to get hurt if this fighting doesn't stop." So, he went to see his nephew. "We've got to stop fighting. Look, we've got all this land around us. Why don't we go our separate ways? Then there will be plenty of food and water for our animals."

"You're right," Lot agreed. He looked around at the wide open countryside. The land around the Jordan River looked like a garden. There would be plenty of food there for his animals. He knew that the land farther away was more like a desert. It would be harder to find food and water there.

"I'll stay here," Lot announced. Abram didn't say a word. He just packed up his tent and his animals and people moved away from the Jordan River. "Abram," God whispered, "look around you. I'm going to give all this land to you someday. You will have as many children as there are stars in the sky. I'm going to bless you, Abram."

Based on Genesis 13

GOD WILL BLESS ABRAM

Becoming a Woman of God
A Woman of God seeks peace.

Abram could have argued with Lot because he wanted the best land. After all, he was older and Lot should have let him have first choice of where to live. But, Abram didn't fight with Lot. It was more important to him to have peace with his nephew. It was a better example of God's love. He knew that God would take care of him, wherever he was.

How good are you at living peacefully with other people? Do you ever argue with your brothers or sisters? Do you fight with your friends? Do you always want to have your own way? What do you learn from Abram about this kind of behavior?

Dad's Turn

Talk about how you got along with your siblings or friends when you were a child. Did you have a brother or a friend with whom you were very competitive? How did that affect your relationship?

Talk to your daughter about how she relates to others. Recall a time when she went out of her way to be peaceful with someone who was being selfish. Congratulate her on her behavior. Talk about what situations make her angry or impatient. Talk about how to handle those feelings.

A Verse to Remember

Live in harmony and peace.

2 Corinthians 13:11

A Baby Named Laughter

Gen. 18:1-15, 21:1-7

Sarah busily cooked up a special dinner. She enjoyed cooking dinner for people. Her husband, Abraham, was outside talking with three men who had dropped by.

Sarah didn't know them, but that didn't matter, a good hostess always offered dinner to travelers.

Then, Sarah heard one of the strangers say something that stopped her in her tracks.

"Haa, haa, haa," Sarah laughed so hard that she dropped the spoon in her hand. She had to grab a chair to keep from falling right down. "That man thinks I'm going to have a baby! Me? Me— with my gray hair, bad eyesight, wrinkled skin? Me??? I'm too old to have a baby!"

The men sitting outside with Abraham looked toward
the tent. "Why did Sarah laugh at our news? God is the
one giving you this baby. Is anything too hard for God?"
Poor Abraham didn't know what to say. God had
promised them a family a long time ago. But, now he
and Sarah were so old . . . it just didn't make any sense.

A few months later Sarah wasn't laughing anymore.
Each time she felt the baby move inside her, she was
amazed. "Put your hand here," she cried, grabbing
Abraham's hand. She laid it on her bulging tummy and
giggled as the baby kicked against it.

When their son was born, Abraham and Sarah named him Isaac, because that name means laughter. Sarah wrapped Isaac in a soft blanket and gently rocked him. "Your father and I have quite a story to tell you," she whispered, "you are a gift from God. A precious gift from God!"

Based on Genesis 18:1-15; 21:1-7

42

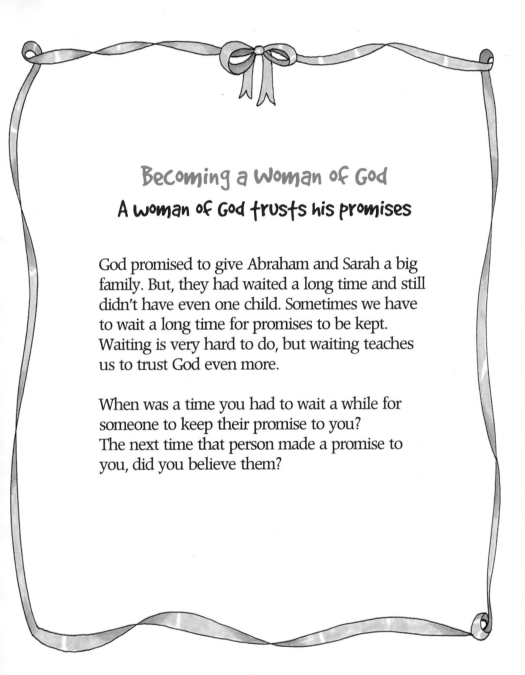

Becoming a Woman of God
A Woman of God trusts his promises

God promised to give Abraham and Sarah a big family. But, they had waited a long time and still didn't have even one child. Sometimes we have to wait a long time for promises to be kept. Waiting is very hard to do, but waiting teaches us to trust God even more.

When was a time you had to wait a while for someone to keep their promise to you?
The next time that person made a promise to you, did you believe them?

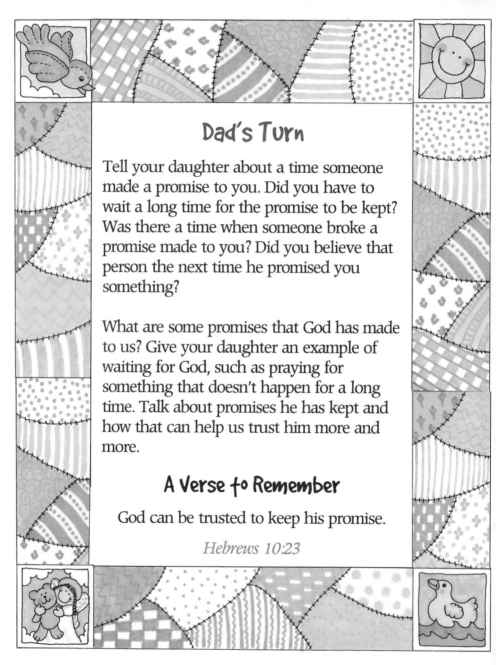

Dad's Turn

Tell your daughter about a time someone made a promise to you. Did you have to wait a long time for the promise to be kept? Was there a time when someone broke a promise made to you? Did you believe that person the next time he promised you something?

What are some promises that God has made to us? Give your daughter an example of waiting for God, such as praying for something that doesn't happen for a long time. Talk about promises he has kept and how that can help us trust him more and more.

A Verse to Remember

God can be trusted to keep his promise.

Hebrews 10:23

The Hardest Test

Gen. 22:1-14

Something didn't feel right, but Sarah couldn't put her finger on what it was. She packed food for Abraham and Isaac to take on their trip to the mountains to make a sacrifice to God.

She made sure Isaac had warm clothes, "It gets cold up in the mountains," she reminded him. But, as they disappeared from sight she realized what was bothering her-Abraham hadn't taken a lamb for the sacrifice! A whisper of fear crept into her heart.

For days Sarah could do nothing but pray, reminding God that Isaac was his gift to her and Abraham in their old age. Several times a day she peeked out the window to see if her husband and son were coming down the path. When she finally saw Isaac skipping down the path ahead of his father, her heart melted in relief and joy.

Home Sweet Home♥

"Momma, wait til you hear," words spilled from Isaac as he climbed onto her lap. "Father tied me up cause I was going to be the sacrifice to God," Sarah's eyes jerked to her husband, but he just pointed her back to Isaac. "Listen to the rest of the story," he seemed to be saying. Sarah knew that her husband trusted God completely, so she turned her attention back to Isaac.

"Just when Father was about to . . . well, an angel stopped him. Now I know that you love God more than anything else," the angel said. "Then he showed us a ram stuck in the bushes. So we caught it and sacrificed it to God. Isn't that cool?"

"Yes, Isaac, that's wonderful. God is good, isn't he?" Sarah hugged her precious son and silently thanked God for his precious love.

Based on Genesis 22:1-14

Becoming a woman of God
A woman of God loves God most of all.

Abraham learned a very hard lesson in this story. He had waited a long time for Isaac to be born and he loved his son very, very much. But Abraham and Sarah both learned that nothing can ever be more important than God.

Is there anything in your life that is sometimes more important to you than God is? It could be a thing or a person or a friendship. Think about how to put that thing in second place . . . right behind God in importance.

Dad's Turn

First, tell your daughter how very much you love her and thank God that she is your daughter.

Tell your daughter about something that was very important to you when you were a boy. Perhaps it was a friend, or sports or the neighborhood you lived in. Was it the most important thing in your life? More important than doing what God wanted? How did you get things in perspective?

A Verse to Remember

Love the LORD your God, walk in all his ways, obey his commands, be faithful to him.

Joshua 22:5

Genesis 26:18-25 ♥

"My Daddy built this well. The Philistines closed it after he died and I think it's time to reopen it," Isaac announced. His servants worked hard to dig out the dirt that plugged up the well.

"Yahoo! Water for us and our herds!" Isaac's workers cheered. But their happiness didn't last long. Men who worked for Gerar ran up shouting, "This is our land, so this well you just dug belongs to us."

"Fight for our well," Isaac's men shouted. But, Isaac didn't want to fight. He took his men and his herds and moved to a new place.

"Dig another well here," he told his men. Once again the men dug a well and cheered when they had fresh water. But again, Gerar's men came and claimed the well.

Isaac and his men moved again and dug a third well. "I hope he doesn't let those creeps take this well, too," Isaac's men grumbled. They wanted to celebrate the fresh cool water, but they were afraid to be too happy.

Isaac studied the horizon, watching for Gerar's men to come and argue about this well, too. One day passed, then two - no one came. Finally, Isaac felt that it was safe to celebrate. "This is where God wants us to stay," he announced.

While Isaac's men tossed water in the air, shouting and celebrating, Isaac thanked God. "I will bless you, Isaac," God promised. "You will have more descendants than you can even imagine!"

Based on Genesis 26:18-25

Becoming a Woman of God

A woman of God chooses her battles.

Isaac was the son of Abraham, a great man of God. All his life Isaac had watched how Abraham lived his life. He saw him stand up and hold his ground when he needed to and he probably saw him sometimes turn and walk away from a fight. He saw that Abraham loved God and lived for him every day. A child learns a lot by watching how his dad lives.

Even though Isaac's workers pushed him to fight for their wells, Isaac knew that wasn't the right thing to do. This wasn't the right time to fight. At some time in life, everybody faces a bully who tries to take what's not theirs. Isaac knew how to handle this instance.

Dad's Turn

Can you share an example of a time when you resisted the urge to fight for something? Were you later glad that you did? How did the problem get solved? Did you talk it through with the other person, or just walk away?

Tell your daughter about a time when you did stand firm and fight for something you believed in or something you owned. Talk to your daughter about bullies she may meet someday who will try to push her around or take her things. Help her plan out gentle (but firm) ways to handle these situations. Help her understand that fighting isn't always the best (or safest) way to handle problems.

A Verse to Remember

The LORD is my strength and my song; he has become my victory.

Exodus 15:2

Moving On

"Joseph is getting on my nerves. He always thinks he's right and he tattles to Dad about every little thing," Joseph's brothers, all ten of them, were fed up to HERE with him.

"Yeah, and Dad doesn't even try to hide that he likes Joseph best. Just look at that fancy coat he gave him. None of us have anything like that! Aahh, he makes me so mad!"

Made Especially for Joseph

One day all the brothers were out in the field. "Psst," whispered one, "look at that bunch of guys coming down the street. They give me an idea. We could sell Joseph to them to be a slave, and just tell Dad that some wild animal ate him."

"Gulp!" Joseph didn't like the way the conversation was heading.

Next thing Joseph knew, he was a slave in Egypt. Things couldn't get much worse . . . then someone lied about him and he landed in jail! He could have sat in the dark with rats crawling around him and been mad at God. But he didn't, his faith grew stronger . . . even though other prisoners made fun of him. "Hey kid, you pray every day-have you noticed that you're still in jail? Maybe your prayers can't get through the walls here!"

A couple of years later, the pharaoh of Egypt had dreams he couldn't understand. "A prisoner named Joseph can explain dreams," someone told him. Right away, Joseph was brought to him . . . and he explained the pharaoh's dreams. Pharaoh was so happy that he made Joseph second in command in the land.

Then there was a terrible drought in the land. No food and no water to drink. Things were tough-except in Egypt where Joseph had planned ahead and stored up water and food. People came  from everywhere to buy food from Joseph. One day, his brothers came. (They didn't recognize him!) Joseph could have said, "No food for you guys! You can starve after what you did to me!" But, he didn't, he knew that the right thing to do was to forgive his brothers and forget their meanness. He sold them food and brought them to live with him in Egypt!

Based on Genesis 37, 39-45

Becoming a Woman of God
A Woman of God forgives others.

If anyone ever had a reason to be mad at
someone, Joseph did. His brothers did a terrible
thing-selling him into slavery and lying to his
dad about what happened to him. But, what
good would it do for Joseph to keep holding a
grudge against them?

It's good to remember that God forgives us for
wrong things we do . . . so we should forgive
others when they hurt us.

Dad's Turn

Dad, has anyone ever forgiven you? Tell your daughter about a time when you really messed up, and the person you hurt forgave you. How did you feel before being forgiven? Afterwards?

Have you ever been able to forgive someone who has hurt you? Tell your daughter about the struggle to forgive. Was it easy or hard?

Is there someone your daughter needs to forgive? Talk to her about how much better she will feel if she can forgive and let go of her anger.

A Verse to Remember

Your love for one another will prove to the world that you are my disciples.

John 13:35

Where There's A Will, There's A Way

Exodus 2:1-10

"Momma, what if Pharaoh's soldiers find our baby? What will they do to him?" Miriam had heard their neighbors talking about Pharaoh's orders–ALL HEBREW BABY BOYS MUST BE KILLED! Now that she had a brand new baby brother, that order sounded really serious.

"I don't care what Pharaoh ordered," Jochebed snapped as she hugged Moses tightly. "I have a plan to keep Moses safe. But, I need your help, Miriam." The big sister was happy to do whatever she could. Jochebed shoved Moses into Miriam's arms and said, "Keep him quiet."

"I'm not going to let them take my son," Jochebed thought as she hurried to the river and picked grass reeds. Walking home carrying a bundle of reeds, she tried not to draw attention to herself. Once inside the house she wove the green reeds into a small basket. Miriam held the baby and wondered what on earth her mom was doing.

"OK, give me the baby," Jochebed held out her arms. She drew Moses close and kissed the top of his head. His fuzzy hair tickled her cheek and he smelled clean and powdery. "Take care of this boy, God," Jochebed prayed as she tucked Moses into the little basket.

"Momma, here's his blanket," Miriam whispered. She wasn't sure what was happening, but she trusted her mom to do what was best for Moses.

Miriam hid by the river, watching Moses' basket boat float away. When a princess opened the basket and picked up Moses, Miriam knew everything was going to be all right. A few minutes later she burst into the house, "Momma, come quick! Pharaoh's daughter found Moses. She's going to keep him, but she wants a Hebrew nurse for him!"

"Praise God!" Jochebed prayed, as she ran to volunteer to take care of her own son!

Based on Exodus 2:1-10

Becoming a Woman of God
A Woman of God does what she can.

Moms and dads love their kids very much. They will do just about anything they can to take care of them. Jochebed took quite a chance by keeping Moses hidden, but she didn't care. Her baby was most important to her, so she did what she could to keep him safe.

When we see something that needs to be done, Jochebed is a good example to jump in and do what we can: ask for God's direction, then get busy!

Dad's Turn

Have you ever gotten involved in a cause . . . saw something that needed to be done, or someone who needed help . . . so you just did it? Tell your daughter about the situation. How did you feel after you had helped? What were you able to do?

Talk to your daughter about ways she could get involved in doing something. Could she do some yard work for an elderly neighbor? Collect canned goods for a neighborhood food pantry? Entertain a younger sibling to help out mom? Pray together that God will show you both ways to get involved.

A Verse to Remember

Are you called to help others? Do it with all the strength and energy that God supplies.

1 Peter 4:11

"**M**omma, why can't I play with my friends?"

No Need for  Water Wings?

Exodus 11:1 – 15:21

Miriam hugged her daughter. She didn't want to ever let her go. When Moses told her that something terrible was going to happen to the Egyptians, Miriam's heart ached for them.

"Why didn't Pharaoh just listen to God?" she thought. "God just wanted him to let us leave Egypt. He's so stubborn . . . now every firstborn child is going to die . . . even Pharaoh's son."

That night
things happened
just as God said they
would. The oldest child in
every Egyptian home died.
Finally, after living through
nine plagues, this tenth one
was the end, Pharaoh begged
the Hebrews to leave. Tears ran
down Miriam's cheeks as she
walked past the Egyptian homes-
heartbroken cries rang from
every door. "Keep looking at the
cloud, Miriam. That's how we
know God is with us," Moses
knew this was hard for his
tenderhearted sister.

Sometimes all that kept the people going as they stumbled through the desert heat, was watching the pillar of fire at night and smoke in the daytime, "God is with us. He's leading us," people would say. Finally, they set up camp on the shore of the Red Sea. Miriam was glad to rest for awhile. But then, she noticed a cloud of dust off in the distance, coming closer and closer. "Pharaoh's army is chasing us!" someone shouted. "Oh no, what will Moses do now?" Miriam wondered.

Moses climbed up on a rock by the water, "Watch what God will do for you!" he shouted. No one paid much attention to him, until the waters began to roll and part into two big walls-with a dry pathway in the middle!

Miriam grabbed her children and followed the other Hebrews through the Red Sea. Every single Hebrew crossed safely. "The Egyptians are following us into the sea," someone shouted. Just then, the water walls rolled together, and every soldier died. "We're safe! Praise God!" Miriam grabbed a tambourine and joined her friends in a dance of victory!

Based on Exodus 11:1-15:21

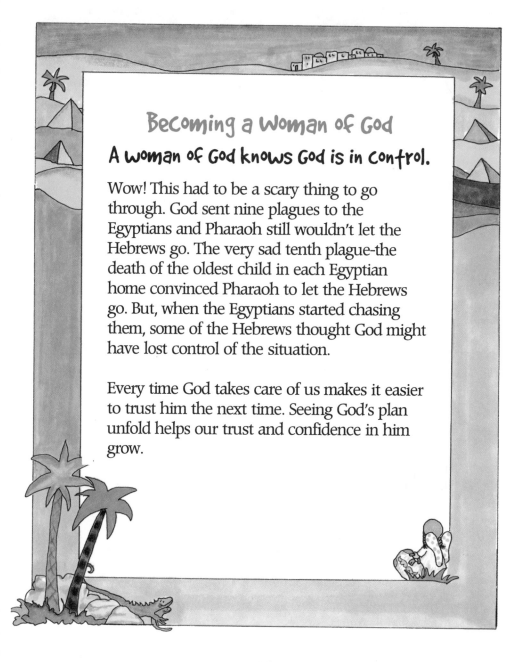

Becoming a Woman of God

A woman of God knows God is in control.

Wow! This had to be a scary thing to go through. God sent nine plagues to the Egyptians and Pharaoh still wouldn't let the Hebrews go. The very sad tenth plague-the death of the oldest child in each Egyptian home convinced Pharaoh to let the Hebrews go. But, when the Egyptians started chasing them, some of the Hebrews thought God might have lost control of the situation.

Every time God takes care of us makes it easier to trust him the next time. Seeing God's plan unfold helps our trust and confidence in him grow.

Dad's Turn

What is the scariest thing that ever happened to you? Why was it frightening? After it was over, did you think about how God helped you or protected you? Were you able to see how this experience was part of God's bigger plan?

Explain to your daughter how going through hard times makes us stronger. Help her remember specific ways God has taken care of your family.

A Verse to Remember

Don't worry about anything; instead pray about everything.

Philippians 4:6

"Come on. We can't stand here all day!" Moses called. He was a man on a mission-leading the Israelites to the land God had promised to them. He didn't have time to stare at the Egyptians soldiers sinking in the Red Sea. Soon a long parade of people was marching toward the Shur Desert. Children walked together, playing on the way, women giggled and whispered as they followed-only Moses marched with purpose.

"Let's Go!"

"Moses, the people are thirsty. You've got to find water for them!" Miriam was elected the spokesman, since Moses was her brother.

"We're in a desert, where do you think I'm going to find water? Besides, I'm thirsty, too." It seemed to Moses like the people complained about everything, forgetting all that God had done to free them from slavery.

Moses led his people farther into the desert. They walked for three days with no water . . . and complained every step of the way. Finally, at Marah they found a pool of cool, ice blue water. "Yippee! Yahoo!" people crowded around and began scooping the water into their mouths.

"YUCK! PHOOEY! This water is bitter. We can't drink this. Are you trying to kill us? What are you going to do about this?" they shouted at Moses.

"God! Help me. Things are getting ugly down here! The people are about to turn on me," Moses cried in desperation.

"Pick up that branch and throw it in the water," God answered. Moses saw the branch beside a rock, but he didn't see how a tree branch could help things, With a mighty heave Moses tossed the branch into the pool of yucky water.

Then, one brave woman dipped her finger in for a small taste. "Yummmm, it's sweet now. Drink up everyone!"

Based on Exodus 15:22-25

Becoming a Woman of God
A woman of God turns to God for help.

Moses was leading the people to the promised land-a job God had given him to do. When the millions of people got angry, they focused their anger on Moses. After all, they couldn't get angry at God. Moses may have wanted to turn and run far away from the Hebrews, but he had a job to do and he was going to do it. So, he prayed for God's help and God helped him, just as he always did.

Dad's Turn

Have you ever been really hungry or thirsty? How did it feel? Have you ever run a long race on a warm day and longed for a cool drink of water? It's not very comfortable to be hot and thirsty, is it?

Tell your daughter about a time when you turned to God for help. What kind of help did you need? How did he help you? Did that experience make it easier to turn to God the next time you needed help?

A Verse to Remember

Give all your worries and cares to God, for he cares about what happens to you.

1 Peter 5:7

"Joshua," Moses called. "We've got a problem! There are some soldiers hiding over there and they don't look too friendly."

"That's because they are from the Amalek army-our worst enemies!" Joshua cried.

"Call your soldiers. We're going to beat them this time!" Moses commanded.

The next morning Moses stood on the top of a big hill and
held his arms out wide-his shepherd's staff pointing to
heaven. Joshua's army fought and fought. Even though the
Amalek army was bigger and definitely meaner, Joshua's
soldiers were winning!

"Ohhh, my arms," Moses moaned. "It feels like my staff weighs 500 pounds." His arms slowly dropped down to his sides-but when they did, the Amalek army started winning! It seemed like Joshua's soldiers couldn't do anything right.

"Help me!" Moses cried. Aaron and Hur ran to
Moses and stood on each side of him. They held
his arms high in the air-and Joshua's army won!
They beat the bigger, meaner Amalek army!

"Yahoo! Yippee! We won! We won!" the soldiers shouted and gave each other high fives as the Amalek army ran away. Moses celebrated, too, he even had enough energy to lift his staff now. Moses built an altar and named it, "The Lord is my banner" and all the Israelites thanked God for his help.

Based on Exodus 17:8-16

Becoming a Woman of God
A woman of God is part of a team.

Joshua's army would have lost the battle if Moses couldn't have held his staff up-it was a sign that God was with them. And, Moses wouldn't have been able to hold his staff up until the battle was over if Aaron and Hur hadn't helped him. Winning this battle definitely took a team effort.

Have you ever been part of a team? If you have played a sport you've probably been on a team where everyone has to work together to win the game. Maybe you've been part of a choir-that's the same thing because everyone must follow the director and work together to make pretty music. It feels good to work with others to accomplish a goal.

Dad's Turn

Tell your daughter about a team you've been part of. How did the members of the team work together to accomplish the goal. Was one person the "star" of the team, how did others help this person do his job? Or, if there wasn't a star how did the team effort work?

Talk with your daughter about the team effort of being part of a family-how each family member is important to keeping the home running smoothly. Talk about other groups your daughter is part of and how she is important to those groups.

A Verse to Remember

Two people can accomplish more than twice as much as one; they get a better return for their labor.

Ecclesiastes 4:9

Exodus 18:5, 19:1, 20:21

"Three months we've walked! Three months! Ever since we left Egypt, we have walked! Are we ever going to get where we're going?" Zipporah dipped her feet into the bucket of cool water. "I think I just saw steam rising from my hot feet," she sighed. At least they had set up camp now. Mt. Sinai rose into the sky right behind them.

After Zipporah cleaned up from supper, she gladly tumbled into bed. Moses came in and tossed some things into a bag. "God called me. I'm going up the mountain," he told her.

"Now? Can't you wait until morning? You must be even more tired than I am," Zipporah knew Moses was responsible for the Israelites, but she worried because he never got any rest. He was always so busy!

A few days later Moses came down the mountain and announced, "God wants to speak to everyone." Three days later, millions of Israelites stood together at the foot of the mountain, anxious to hear what God would say. Thunder so loud that it shook the ground crashed all around the mountain. Lightning flashed across the sky. Zipporah was so nervous that she could barely catch her breath.

Some people around her dropped to their knees in worship. Being in the presence of the awesome God was frightening. Zipporah had new respect for her husband, who was often called into God's presence. She looked up to see Moses climbing the mountain once again, disappearing into the clouds for a personal meeting with God.

Moses was gone for a long time. Zipporah began to wonder if she would ever see him again, "God, I know that you love Moses, even more than I do. Take care of him and bring him back safely."

When Moses finally came back he was carrying two huge stone tablets. "God himself wrote these ten rules for us to live by," Moses told the people. Ten simple rules on how to treat God and one another.

Based on Exodus 18:5; 19:1-20:21

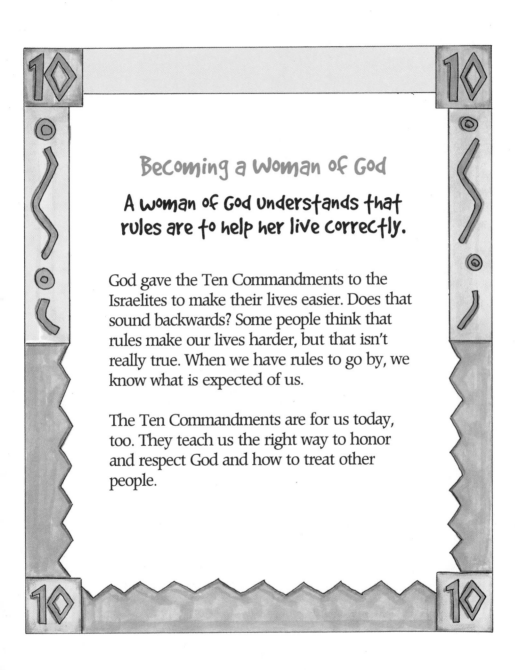

Becoming a Woman of God

A woman of God understands that rules are to help her live correctly.

God gave the Ten Commandments to the Israelites to make their lives easier. Does that sound backwards? Some people think that rules make our lives harder, but that isn't really true. When we have rules to go by, we know what is expected of us.

The Ten Commandments are for us today, too. They teach us the right way to honor and respect God and how to treat other people.

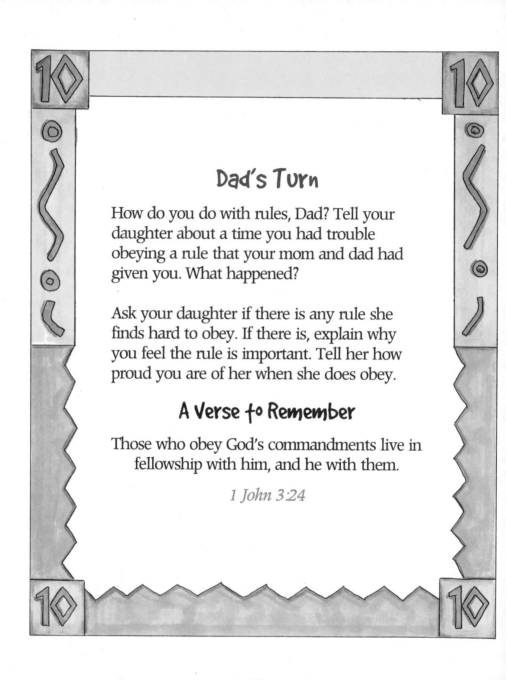

Dad's Turn

How do you do with rules, Dad? Tell your daughter about a time you had trouble obeying a rule that your mom and dad had given you. What happened?

Ask your daughter if there is any rule she finds hard to obey. If there is, explain why you feel the rule is important. Tell her how proud you are of her when she does obey.

A Verse to Remember

Those who obey God's commandments live in fellowship with him, and he with them.

1 John 3:24

Grapeland

Numbers 13-14

"Last, but not least, I choose Caleb and Joshua. You twelve men will sneak into the land of Canaan," Moses announced. "God wants you to check out the land. Is the soil good? Do good crops grow there? Do the towns have walls? Are the armies big?" Moses gave instructions to the men who were running around trying to get organized.

One afternoon the spies were carefully picking their way down the side of a mountain. "Careful, don't slip!" someone called. When all twelve were safely down the men took a minute to look around.

"Look at the size of those grapes!" one man whispered. "I've never seen anything like this. Let's cut a cluster and take it back to show everyone."

Forty days after leaving on their special mission, the twelve men returned to Moses and reported. "Wonderful crops grow in Canaan-just look at these huge grapes. It's a beautiful land, with lots of space for us and plenty of food and water."

"Yeah, but on the other hand, the people there are giants . . . I mean GIANTS! And the cities have big walls around them," another man said.

The spies argued among themselves about whether or not the Israelites should try to capture the land. Two spies-Joshua and Caleb-said, "Let's go for it. God already said that the land is ours!" But, the other ten were chicken because of the giants.

The people listened to the spies argue and finally someone said, "I agree with the ten-there's no way we could capture Canaan." The whole crowd sided with the ten who were chicken. Caleb and Joshua were very frustrated.

God was even more frustrated that Caleb and Joshua. "I told you that I was giving you the land. Since you don't believe me-you will wander around for forty years (one year for every day the spies were gone). After that I'll give you this land-but none of you will be alive to see it-except Caleb and Joshua, who believed me."

Based on Numbers 13-14

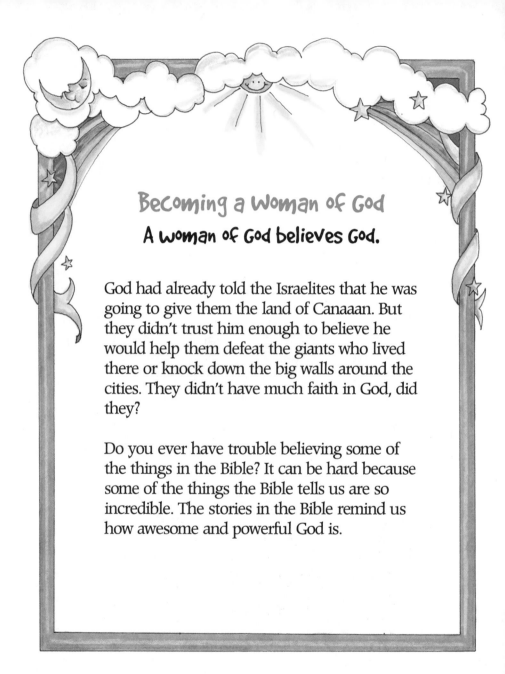

Becoming a Woman of God

A woman of God believes God.

God had already told the Israelites that he was going to give them the land of Canaaan. But they didn't trust him enough to believe he would help them defeat the giants who lived there or knock down the big walls around the cities. They didn't have much faith in God, did they?

Do you ever have trouble believing some of the things in the Bible? It can be hard because some of the things the Bible tells us are so incredible. The stories in the Bible remind us how awesome and powerful God is.

Dad's Turn

Do you easily believe new things? Or are you from Missouri—the "SHOW ME" state? Tell your daughter about something you once found difficult to believe. Perhaps the whole concept of heaven was difficult to grasp. Or maybe there are other things in our world that are so amazing to you that they are difficult to believe.

Ask your daughter if there is anything that she has trouble understanding and therefore believing. Perhaps you can explain that thing so simply that she understands it.

A Verse to Remember

What is faith? It is the confident assurance that what we hope for is going to happen.

Hebrews 11:1

Showdown at the Old Oak Tree

Judges 6:1-24

"God, save us!" the Israelite people prayed day after day. They sort of forgot that the reason they were having so many problems was because they kept disobeying God. "Our enemies are so mean that we have to hide in the mountains. We've lost our homes, our cattle, our crops. God, we're starving!"

God heard their cries and sent an angel to sit beneath an old oak tree where Gideon was secretly threshing wheat. He was going to hide it from their enemies. "Mighty hero, the LORD is with you!" the angel said.

"Oh right," Gideon snapped. "If God is with us, then why are we having so many problems?"

"God is sending you to rescue the people," the angel answered.

"Gulp!" Gideon didn't know what to think about that. "Whoa, that can't be-I'm a nobody-surely I'm not the best choice. I'm going to need some proof that God really wants me for this job."

The angel waited patiently while Gideon hurried home to cook a goat and bake some bread. When he returned, the angel said, "Put it on that rock over there and pour broth over it."

"Stand back!" the angel shouted. He touched the dripping
meat and bread with his staff and fire shot out from the rock.
Every drop of meat, bread and gravy burned right up. Now
Gideon knew that God wanted him to do this job.

Based on Judges 6:1-24

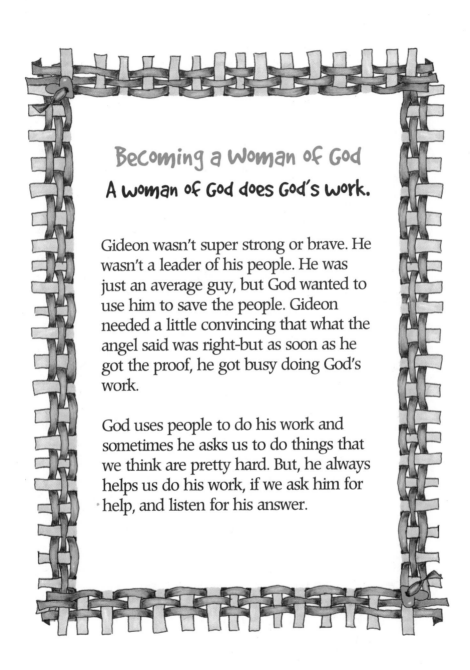

Becoming a Woman of God
A Woman of God does God's work.

Gideon wasn't super strong or brave. He wasn't a leader of his people. He was just an average guy, but God wanted to use him to save the people. Gideon needed a little convincing that what the angel said was right-but as soon as he got the proof, he got busy doing God's work.

God uses people to do his work and sometimes he asks us to do things that we think are pretty hard. But, he always helps us do his work, if we ask him for help, and listen for his answer.

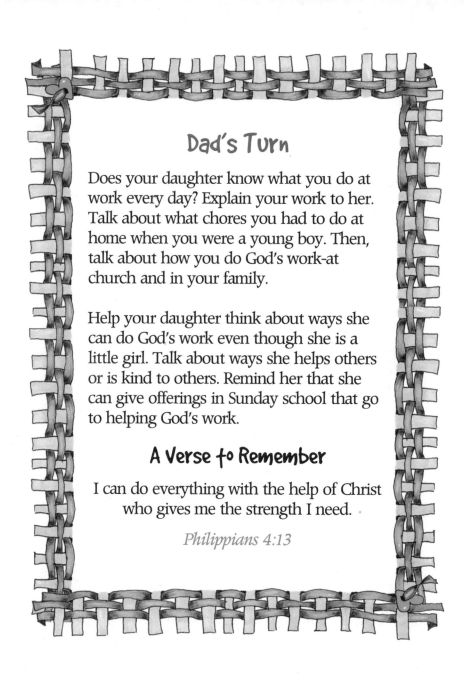

Dad's Turn

Does your daughter know what you do at work every day? Explain your work to her. Talk about what chores you had to do at home when you were a young boy. Then, talk about how you do God's work-at church and in your family.

Help your daughter think about ways she can do God's work even though she is a little girl. Talk about ways she helps others or is kind to others. Remind her that she can give offerings in Sunday school that go to helping God's work.

A Verse to Remember

I can do everything with the help of Christ who gives me the strength I need.

Philippians 4:13

"Gideon, I'm tired of Israel worshipping other gods. Help me put a stop to it-tear down your dad's altar to Baal and cut down the Asherah pole that's next to it. Build an altar to me in it's place," God said.

"Everyone in town worships Baal. If I knock down their altar, they're going to be really mad," Gideon was a little nervous.

But God didn't change his request. So, Gideon waited until it was dark and everyone was sleeping. He ordered his servants, "Pull down this altar, stone by stone. Don't leave one stone in place." While they worked on that Gideon cut down the Asherah pole. But, the whole time he kept looking around to make sure no one was coming.

When the altar was down, Gideon built an altar to God. Heaving a big bull onto it, he sacrificed it to God. "Father, thank you for loving us. Forgive your people once again for turning away from you." As the sun peeked over the horizon, Gideon tumbled into bed.

Father, forgive your people again for turning away from you

Father, thank you for forgiving us

It didn't take long the next morning for people to notice what had happened, "Hey, what happened to Baal's altar?" "Yeah, and to the Asherah pole? Who would do this?"

"Someone built a new altar and sacrificed a bull to God." Quickly a mob started looking for the person who had done this. The evidence pointed to Gideon.

"Give us your son. He's going to pay for this!" the mob shouted at Joash. "He wrecked Baal's altar!" Gideon hid behind a door and prayed.

His dad looked around at his friends and neighbors before saying, "Why are you fighting Baal's battle? If he's really so powerful, let him rebuild his altar and take care of my son. Maybe we should be worshipping the real God instead of a fake one."

Based on Judges 6:25-32

Becoming a Woman of God
A woman of God takes a stand for him.

God asked Gideon to do something pretty hard, didn't he? Gideon took a stand for God when he knew that the rest of the people were not going to like it. They might have gotten really angry at Gideon and chased him out of town . . . or hurt him. But, Gideon did what God asked, because that's how important God was to him.

Have you ever stood up for something that you believe is right, even if your friends don't agree with you? Were you glad that you did?

Dad's Turn

Have you ever stood firm in your faith, even when friends were tempting you not to? Tell your daughter about a time when you resisted going along with the crowd. How did it turn out? Perhaps you can share about a time when you did do what the gang wanted and then regretted it.

Talk with your daughter about the temptation of doing what everyone else does, even when you know it isn't the right thing to do. Give her suggestions on how to stand up for what is right, even if it isn't the popular thing to do.

A Verse to Remember

Always keep your conscience clear.

1 Timothy 1:19

1 SAMUEL 16:13

"Naa naa naa na naa ya, we're going to meet Samuel the priest and you're not!" David's older brother loved to tease him. "You're just a baby-only good for taking care of the sheep. We OLDER brothers have more important things to do."

"He's only a little bit older than me," David thought. "I wish I could go to the meeting with Samuel." He turned around to see his father and all seven of his older brothers leaving for town and the meeting with Samuel and all the town leaders. Dragging his staff in the dirt, David headed for the field.

David settled down near his sheep and
began playing his harp. It was peaceful
and quiet on the hillside. Meanwhile at
the meeting in town, Samuel asked to meet David's older
brothers. Eliab, the oldest, came to Samuel. He was tall and
strong and very handsome. Samuel seemed excited to meet
him, but after a few minutes of silence, he asked to meet
the next boy.

Soon Samuel had met all of the boys. He seemed to be looking for something or someone . . . but he didn't find it with any of them. Turning to Jesse, he asked, "Do you have any other sons?"

"Well, my youngest is at home watching the sheep. But, he's just a little tyke, why would you care about him?" Jesse answered.

All Samuel would say was, "Go get him."

As soon as David came into the room, Samuel ran to him and laid his hands on David's small shoulders. "You're the one," he whispered. "God has told me that you will be king of Israel. I am here to anoint you." David was filled with joy as Samuel poured the anointing oil on his head. God hadn't chosen any of his older, taller, stronger, handsomer brothers-God chose David.

Based on 1 Samuel 16:1-13

Becoming a Woman of God

A Woman of God may be a child.

David's older brother wasn't too nice, was he? He thought that David wasn't worth much because he was just a little guy. But, God doesn't look at how big or strong we are. He doesn't care if we're pretty or handsome. God looks at our hearts. He looks to see if we love him and want to serve him. He looks to see if we care about other people. Even a child can have a heart that loves God.

Dad's Turn

When did you come to faith in God? Were you a young person or an adult? If you were a child, tell your daughter about the experience. Tell her ways you got involved in God's work as a young person.

Help your daughter see ways that she can serve God as a young person. Plan a family time of serving at an inner city ministry or food pantry. Show her the practical ways of helping others and serving God.

A Verse to Remember

Don't let anyone think less of you because you are young. Be an example to all believers in what you teach, in the way you live, in your love, your faith, and your purity.

1 Timothy 4:12

A STONE'S THROW

"You're always acting like such a big shot. Why don't you just go home?" Eliab shoved his little brother and David tumbled to the ground.

"Father sent me here to bring this stuff to you guys," David tried to explain. "I was just looking around. I've never seen an army camp before."

"How come none of King Saul's soldiers will fight that Philistine giant, Goliath?" he continued. But Eliab didn't answer, he just stomped away.

Just then David heard Goliath shouting again, "Hey, you Israelite chickens. Send someone out to fight me! Come on, don't you think your big, powerful God will help you?"

"Ooooo, that creep. How can you guys let him make fun of God like that?" David looked around at the big, strong soldiers. None of them would even look back at him. So, David marched into King Saul's tent and shouted, "I'm just a kid, but I'll fight the giant. Just let me at him!"

King Saul looked at shrimpy little David, then he looked out at the giant Goliath . . . "OK, but at least wear my armor!" he said. But, when David got it on, "Hey, I can't walk . . . I can't even see . . . this stuff is too heavy. Take if off! I'm going to do this my way!" he shouted.

Hurrying down the hill, David stopped to pick up 5 stones. When Goliath saw that a kid was coming to fight him, he got boiling mad! He shouted and stomped and sputtered. "Give it up, Big Guy, you can't win because God is helping me," David thought. He calmly put a stone in his slingshot and swung it around and around. The stone flew through the air and THWACKED into Goliath's head. The earth shook as the giant dropped to the ground, "David won! David won!" King Saul's soldiers shouted.

Based on 1 Samuel 17:1-51

Becoming a Woman of God

A Woman of God fights in God's strength.

David knew that he wasn't fighting alone. He knew that a little kid like him wouldn't have a chance against a nine foot tall giant soldier like Goliath-except that God was helping him. That was something that King Saul's soldiers didn't understand, or one of them would have fought the giant.

When you have Christ living in your heart, you are never alone. He will help you with the tough things you may have to do, if you just ask him.

Dad's Turn

Recall a time when you had to do something that really scared you. Maybe it was public speaking, maybe it was moving to a new state-whatever it was, it was not easy! Tell your daughter about it. Tell her why it was scary to you and tell her how you got through it.

Ask your daughter what kinds of things she thinks are frightening. Talk about how to handle those things. Pray together for God's strength to help her do hard things.

A Verse to Remember

For nothing is impossible with God.

Luke 1:37

"Are you Mephibosheth?" a mean-looking soldier growled. For just a minute Mephibosheth thought about saying, "No." After all, why would one of King David's soldiers be looking for him? "Well?" the soldier asked. Mephibosheth knew that this guy wasn't going away so he finally admitted that he was.

"Come with me. King David wants to see you," the soldier said as he turned away.

"Well, this can't be good. Why would King David want to see me? My grandpa, King Saul tried for years to kill King David. So what if the king is going to put me in jail-or do something worse-because of what my grandfather did?" he wondered.

Mephibosheth followed behind the soldier as quickly as he
could. His feet were crippled from a childhood accident so
walking was not easy. The soldier led him right to King David.
Mephibosheth dropped to his knees. He had never been this
close to the famous king. His heart was pounding so hard that he
thought the king must be able to hear it.

King David gently lifted Mephibosheth to his feet. "Your father, Jonathan, was the best friend I've ever had," the king said. "I promised him a long time ago that when I became king I would take care of his children and grandchildren. You're the only one who is still alive. I want to keep my promise to Jonathan." Mephibosheth didn't know what to say, so he just stood there staring at the great king.

"I'd like you to come live here in the palace with me."
Mephibosheth looked around at the grand palace. He had never
seen anything so beautiful. "You can eat all your meals with me.
I will give back to you all the land that once belonged to your
grandfather and I will have someone farm it to grow food for
your family." Mephibosheth was amazed at King David's
kindness. He bowed to the king, thanking him over and over.

Based on 2 Samuel 9

Becoming a Woman of God
A woman of God is kind.

King David didn't have to be kind to Mephibosheth. No one knew about his promise to Jonathan, except him and God. But, King David loved God and tried to live for him. Keeping the promise he had made was one way to show others that God was important to him.

Do you take your promises seriously? Or do you promise, "I'll clean my room after lunch," and then forget about it completely. If you keep your promises, it shows you have an honest heart and that how you treat others is important to you.

Dad's Turn

Have you ever made a promise without really thinking about how difficult it would be to keep it? Did you keep it anyway? Tell your daughter about a time when you kept a promise, even though it wasn't easy for you. Tell her how you felt afterwards.

Help your daughter understand that something as simple as keeping a promise can show others how important God is to us. It's a way of witnessing that God lives in our hearts. Remind her to think before she makes a promise and not to make a promise that she can't keep.

A Verse to Remember

Don't lie to each other.

Colossians 3:9

BIRDFEEDER

A hab was the worst king Israel had ever, ever had. He didn't care a bit about God or any of God's rules for living. He was mean and selfish and cheated people. To make things even worse, he married Jezebel, who worshipped fake gods-so he did, too. Ahab made God more angry than any other king before him. God decided to get Ahab's attention.

"Elijah, tell Ahab that it isn't going to rain in Israel for years until you say so-because I say so!"

"Ahab isn't going to be happy about this!" Elijah was a little worried.

"Don't worry about him," God said, "go hide in the forest by the Kerith Brook. I'll take care of you."

Elijah gave Ahab the God-is-mad-so-it's-not-going-to-rain-for-a-long-time news. Then he ran for his life. He set up camp by Kerith Brook. And waited. Hot sunshine quickly dried up ponds and rivers all around Israel. Elijah knew that people were going hungry and thirsty because there was no rain to make the food grow and no water to drink.

Slurping a drink of cool, clear water from Kerith Brook, Elijah wondered what he was going to do when his food ran out. One morning Elijah woke up to a strange sound. He peeked open an eye to see a big raven nearby with a hunk of bread in it's beak. "Yahoo! Food! God is sending me food!" Elijah shouted.

The next morning Elijah woke up wondering if the raven would come back. Sure enough, every morning and every night the raven brought meat and bread for him. So, Elijah stayed hidden by the Kerith Brook, until all of it's water dried up, too. Then God sent him somewhere else.

Based on 1 Kings 17:1-7

Becoming a Woman of God
A Woman of God is Cared for by God.

God never leaves us to stumble through life by ourselves. He knew that King Ahab was going to be plenty angry at Elijah and even blame Elijah because it didn't rain. So, God took care of Elijah. He sent him to a safe place and provided food and water for him.

It's hard to not worry about things that happen to us . . . or that we are afraid may happen to us. But, stories like this one remind us that God will always take care of us, all we have to do is trust him.

Dad's Turn

When was a time that you worried about something? Maybe there wasn't enough money to pay the bills, or perhaps you lost your job. Did you trust God to meet that need? Have you ever seen God miraculously provide for you? Tell your daughter about it.

Remind your daughter that worrying doesn't help anything . . . it just makes us worry more. Talk about the story of God caring for Elijah and how it can enourage her to trust God to take care of her, too.

A Verse to Remember

Trust in the LORD with all your heart; do not depend on your own understanding.

Proverbs 3:5

"Shhhh! Did you hear something?"

←CAVE

King Ahab and Queen Jezebel were hopping mad! From their viewpoint it made perfect sense, after all, Elijah had killed 400 prophets of the fake god, Baal-the god they worshipped. It sure didn't make them look too good. "I better get out of here," Elijah thought and he headed for the hills . . . actually Mt. Sinai.

Elijah ran and ran, finally collapsing inside a cave tucked away near the top of the mountain. "What are you doing here," a voice rang through the darkness.

Elijah knew it was God's voice. "Look, I've spent my life teaching Israel about you. But, the people break their promises to you, tear down your altars, even kill your prophets. I'm the only one left! I can't take it anymore, I'm hiding here!"

"Go outside. Stand on the mountain," God commanded. Elijah crept just outside the cave opening and looked up at the sky. Suddenly a ferocious wind began to blow. It blew harder and harder until rocks pulled away from the mountain and tumbled down. Elijah held on for dear life. "God," he said, "was I supposed to hear your voice in this powerful wind?"

The earth began to shake and roll as if someone had picked up the mountain and was shaking it as hard as they could. Elijah fell to his knees and held on to a tree trunk. "Is God trying to speak to me now?" he wondered.

Then he heard a hissing sound and looked up to see a wall of fire roaring up the mountain. Dashing back into the cave, Elijah listened for God to speak . . . but he heard nothing.

When the fire passed, Elijah stood up and brushed himself off-this had been quite a day. That's when he heard it . . . a gentle whisper floating up the mountain . . . the voice of God, "You aren't really alone, Elijah. There are still others who love me. Just keep on doing my work."

Based on 1 Kings 19:8-18

Becoming a Woman of God
A Woman of God listens for his voice.

Have you ever noticed how noisy our world is? We learn from Elijah that we should get away from the noise and busyness of our world in order to hear God's voice. He won't try to compete with television noise or noisy playmates. To hear God's voice we need to be in a quiet place for awhile . . . and listen. When God speaks to us, it probably won't be in a voice that sounds like a person, it's more like a whisper inside your heart.

Do you sometimes spend quiet time just listening to the world around you? Do you ever hear God's voice speaking inside your heart?

Dad's Turn

How good are you at being quiet? Do you tend to have the TV or radio on as background noise most of the time? Do an experiment with your daughter. Go outside and sit quietly in the park or your backyard. Don't speak at all, just listen for about 10 minutes. Then talk about the sounds that you heard. Did you hear things that you don't usually notice?

Help your daughter establish a quiet time with God every day. Spend 5 or 10 minutes with her. Pray and read a verse of Scripture, then just be quiet for a few minutes.

A Verse to Remember

You should be known for the beauty that comes from within, the unfading beauty of a gentle and quiet spirit, which is precious to God.

1 Peter 3:4

"Momma, why is that man so mean? He scares me," the little boy grabbed his mom's leg and buried his face in her skirt. His older brother tried to act tougher, but fear shone from his eyes, too. Their mom hugged the boys to her side and watched the man walk away. "My boys are right," she thought, "that man is mean."

Of course, she would never say that out loud. She was a gentle woman who tried to raise her sons to be good men. But, ever since her husband died, the mean man had been threatening her. He said her husband had owed him lots of money and he wanted it . . . NOW! The woman looked around her house-she had sold lots of her furniture-and she still didn't have money to pay the man.

Leaving her sons with a neighbor, the woman hurried across town to see Elisha. "If the prophet of God can't help me, no one can," she thought. Elisha listened as she blurted out her story. He could hear the fear and pain in her voice. "My boys are all I have left. Please don't let him take them," she begged.

Have faith ♥ Elisha will help!

Elisha and the woman hurried to her house. "You have one jar of olive oil here, right?" he asked. She nodded, but thought that was an odd thing to focus on. "Find as many empty jars as you can. Send your sons to borrow some from your neighbors," he ordered. The boys thought this was a great adventure as they hurried from neighbor to neighbor.

"Pour oil into that first jar. Keep filling jars until your own oil jar is empty," Elisha said quietly. The woman didn't even question this odd command. She started pouring oil.

"Boys, bring more jars!" she cried as she filled jar after jar from her one little jar. "Pay attention, sons, you're seeing God take care of us!"

Elisha smiled as he told the woman, "Sell this extra oil. Pay the man and keep whatever money is left over to buy food for your family."

Based on 2 Kings 4:1-7

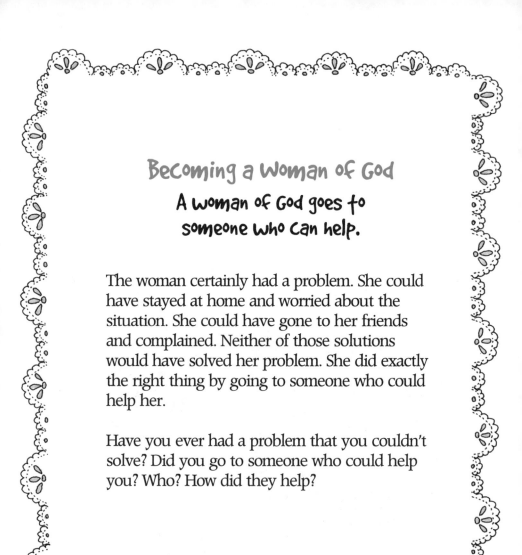

Becoming a Woman of God

A woman of God goes to someone who can help.

The woman certainly had a problem. She could have stayed at home and worried about the situation. She could have gone to her friends and complained. Neither of those solutions would have solved her problem. She did exactly the right thing by going to someone who could help her.

Have you ever had a problem that you couldn't solve? Did you go to someone who could help you? Who? How did they help?

Dad's Turn

We all like to think that we can solve our own problems. Occasionally, however, we all run up against something that we just can't handle—and we need help. Tell your daughter about a time when you had a problem and you tried and tried to solve it yourself. Finally, realizing that you couldn't solve it on your own, you went to someone for help. How did it turn out?

Brainstorm with your daughter the names of some adults who might be available to help her with a problem. Remind her that she should always go to God with her problems, because he cares so very much about her.

A Verse to Remember

God is our refuge and strength, always ready to help in times of trouble.

Psalm 46:1

Elisha came into Shunem tired and hungry. As he traveled from town to town, it was always interesting to see who would invite him to stay at their home or come for dinner. In Shunen, it always seemed to be the same kind lady.

She was a great cook and very generous with the nice home she and her husband shared. She seemed to really enjoy having company. Elisha always looked forward to staying with her. Tonight, this prophet of God needed a good rest.

The next morning Elisha continued on his journey. As the kind woman waved goodbye to him, an idea popped into her head. Later that night, she shared her idea with her husband. "Why don't we build a room onto our house just for Elisha? Then he would have a place to stay anytime he comes to Shunem. He could even leave a few things here if he wants."

Her husband, who was just as generous as she was, thought her idea was a good one! Right away he started measuring and hammering and sawing. The woman looked at curtain fabrics and made cushions for the chair. The room was ready and waiting the next time Elisha came to Shunem.

♥ Thank You God ♥

welcome
Elisha

A few weeks later, Elisha strolled into town and everyone he greeted seemed to be keeping a secret. "I wonder what's going on here," Elisha thought to himself. He soon found out as the kind lady and her husband showed Elisha the new room, built just for him. Elisha gratefully praised God for the generosity and kindness of this couple.

Based on 2 Kings 4:8-11

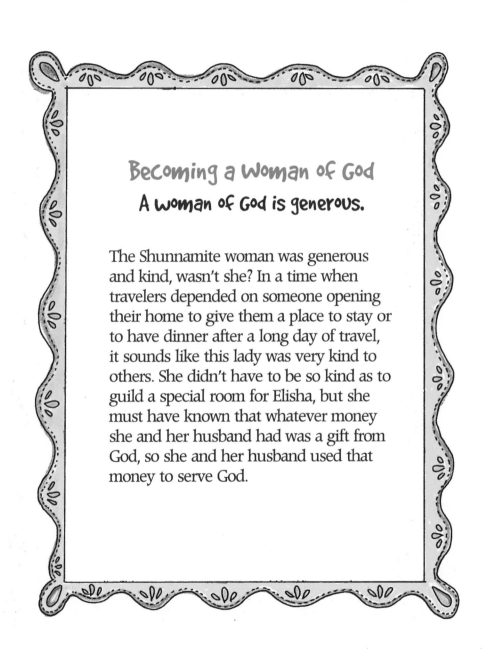

Becoming a Woman of God
A woman of God is generous.

The Shunnamite woman was generous and kind, wasn't she? In a time when travelers depended on someone opening their home to give them a place to stay or to have dinner after a long day of travel, it sounds like this lady was very kind to others. She didn't have to be so kind as to guild a special room for Elisha, but she must have known that whatever money she and her husband had was a gift from God, so she and her husband used that money to serve God.

Dad's Turn

It really makes you feel good when someone goes out of their way to be generous. Can you recall a time when someone did something for you or gave you something that was a generous gift? Can you give an example of a time when you were generous, either with money or with your time?

Help your daughter recognize generosity directed to her—either through gifts or through time spent with her.

A Verse to Remember

All the believers were of one heart and mind, and they felt that what they owned was not their own; they shared everything they had.

Acts 4:32

Beauty AND Bravery

In Esther's mind the last year was just a blur. Special beauty treatments, fancy foods, beautiful clothes. She went from being a simple (although beautiful) Jewish girl . . . to queen of Persia! Everyone loved Esther. She was kind and loving-with a heart just as beautiful as her face.

But, young Queen Esther had a problem. "Haman ordered everyone to bow down to him. I refused, because I will only bow to God," Esther's Uncle Mordecai told her. "Now he has commanded that all the Jews in the country be killed!"

"Uncle, I can't help. No one-not even the king-knows that I am Jewish. You're the one who told me to keep it a secret," Esther was very confused.

"I know, child. But this may be the very reason God made you queen-to save your people!" Mordecai was very convincing.

That night Esther couldn't sleep. She paced around her bedroom. She prayed. She cried. She knew that the king could have her killed if she went to see him without being called. She wondered what would happen when he found out that she was Jewish. Finally, early in the morning, she sent a note to Mordecai: "I'm going to talk to the king. Pray for me-if I die, then I die."

Esther had her hair curled. She put on her prettiest dress and most expensive perfume. Then she invited the king and Haman to a special banquet. The two men laughed and talked as they ate. But, Esther was so nervous that she could barely speak. Finally, just before dessert she blurted out, "Haman is planning to kill me and all my people!"

The king listened silently as Esther explained Haman's plan . . . and her own Jewishness. Her knees crumbled in relief when the king called in his guards to lead Haman away to be hung in the very gallows he had built for Mordecai. The Jewish people were saved, thanks to the courage of the beautiful young queen.

Based on the Book of Esther

Becoming a Woman of God
A woman of God asks others to pray for her.

Esther risked her life by going to the king. He could have had her killed and then the Jewish people would still have died. But, Esther was courageous and did what she could to stop Haman's terrible plan. But, what did Esther do before she went to the king? She asked people to pray for her. She knew that in order to be able to save her people, she needed God's help.

Have you ever asked someone to pray for you about some particular situation? Did you feel better knowing that someone was praying for you?

Dad's Turn

Tell your daughter about a situation you've been through when the prayers of others really helped you. Give her an example of a time you sincerely prayed about something and God answered your prayer.

Help your daughter make a prayer list or journal of requests to bring before God. Pray with her now.

A Verse to Remember

Pray at all times and on every occasion in the power of the Holy Spirit. Stay alert and be persistent in your prayers for all Christians everywhere.

Ephesians 6:18

"Cool . . . steak and potatoes, cake and ice cream. Boy, oh boy, this is the life!" The guys around Daniel leaned back on satin couches and picked their teeth.

"Helloooo . . . we're slaves. We aren't free. Don't get caught up in the fancy food and stuff. This food is offered to their idols before it's given to us. This is more serious than fancy food," Daniel couldn't believe what he was hearing.

"Oh Daniel, you worry too much," one boy snarled before stretching out to take a nap. "You'd probably rather be in a jail cell instead of living in a palace!"

"Isn't anyone with me here?" Daniel asked. His three friends, Shadrach, Meshach and Abednego stepped forward. The four of them went off by themselves to hear Daniel's plan.

"My friends and I don't want this fancy food. Just give us vegetables and water," Daniel told the guard.

"No way, you guys are being trained to serve in King Nebuchadnezzar's palace. If you don't look as healthy as the other prisoners, he'll have my neck," the guard liked Daniel because he was respectful and honest. But, he wasn't willing to take a chance.

"We don't want to get you in trouble. How about a 10 day test? Then if we don't look as good as the other guys, we'll eat your food," Daniel was pretty convincing. So, for 10 days the guard slipped Daniel and his friends broccoli and carrots while the other guys had steak and pastries.

The other boys thought the four "veggie boys" were crazy. "Yumm! You don't know what you're missing!" they waved their fancy foods in Daniel's face.

A strange thing happened during the next ten days. Daniel and his friends grew stronger and healthier than any of the other guys! "It's veggies and water for you guys from now on!" the guard laughed.

At the end of the training, the boys who hadn't honored God were amazed that the king was more impressed with Daniel, Shadrach, Meshach and Abednego than anyone else.

Based on Daniel 1

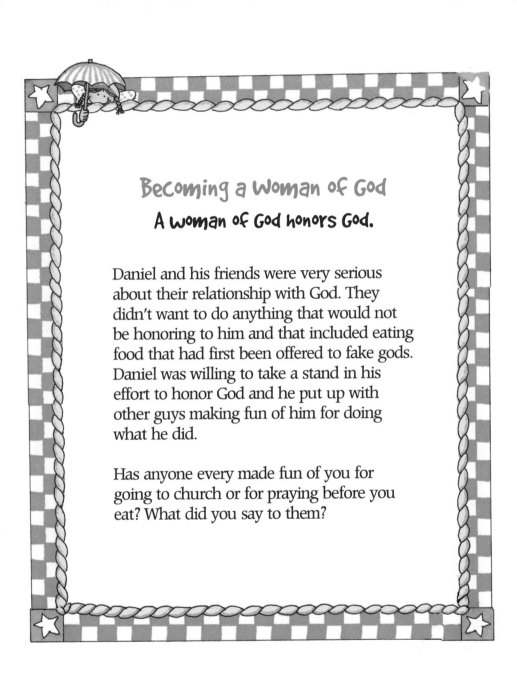

Becoming a Woman of God

A Woman of God honors God.

Daniel and his friends were very serious
about their relationship with God. They
didn't want to do anything that would not
be honoring to him and that included eating
food that had first been offered to fake gods.
Daniel was willing to take a stand in his
effort to honor God and he put up with
other guys making fun of him for doing
what he did.

Has anyone every made fun of you for
going to church or for praying before you
eat? What did you say to them?

Dad's Turn

When you were in high school or college, did anyone ever challenge your stand for God? Did they question why you were so serious about living for him? How did you handle that? If that hasn't happened to you, have you ever experienced peer pressure to behave in a way that you didn't really want to? How did you handle that?

Talk with your daughter about some things in life that are nonnegotiables—ways that a Christian always behaves and can't be justified away. A Christian is honest, kind, loving, peaceful . . . what else?

A Verse to Remember

Do not worship any other gods besides me.

Exodus 20:3

The Birth of the King

Luke 2:1-20

With every bouncing step the donkey took Mary wanted to break down and cry. She was tired, every bone in her body hurt, and the baby in her tummy was wiggling his complaints about the long donkey ride. "If only we didn't have to go to Bethlehem to be counted in the census," she thought.

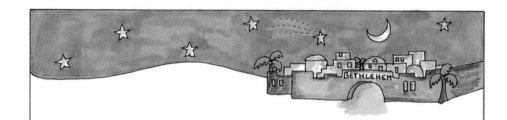

Joseph could have gone alone, but since the baby was due any day Mary didn't want to be away from him. "Are you OK, Mary?" Joseph asked.

She sat up straighter and answered, "Yes, but is it much farther?" She didn't want to worry him, but Mary didn't know how much longer she could ride on this donkey.

"We'll be there soon and we'll get a room with a soft bed so you can rest," Joseph promised.

When they got to Bethlehem, Mary was surprised at the crowded streets. Hundreds of people had come to be counted in the census. She waited while Joseph went to get a room. People pushed past her and animals bellowed. Mary couldn't wait to get inside.

"There aren't any rooms—the whole town is full! The innkeeper said that since you're pregnant, we can stay in his stable. I'm so sorry, but I think it's the best we can do," Joseph apologized.

"It's OK. I just want to lie down," Mary sighed. Sliding from the donkey, she settled down on some clean straw and fell right to sleep. A few hours later a sharp pain shooting through her tummy woke her up. "Joseph . . . the baby. WAKE UP!"

Joseph tried his best to make her comfortable and help in whatever way he could. When he finally laid the newborn baby in her arms, Mary smiled up at him.

Mary wrapped Jesus in a clean blanket and kissed his soft brown hair and pudgy neck. Mary and Joseph sat together and watched in amazement as the new baby slept. "He's the son of God," Mary whispered. "The son of God."

"I know," Joseph whispered back. "God is trusting us to raise his son. This little boy will grow up to be our Savior."

Based on Luke 2:1-20

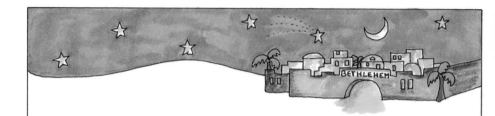

Becoming a Woman of God
A woman of God knows her Savior.

Mary knew Jesus in a way that no one else ever has. She was his earthly mother, but she knew that Jesus would be her Savior, too. Mary was chosen to be Jesus' mother because her heart was so in tune with God. That helped her believe that Jesus wasn't just an ordinary baby.

Do you believe that Jesus is your Savior? Do you understand that you are a sinner and that Jesus died for your sins so you can live in heaven with him someday?

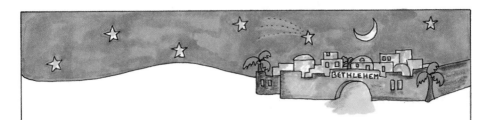

Dad's Turn

Tell your daughter the story of your own salvation. Who led you to the Lord? How did you come to the point of realizing your need for Christ?

Talk to your daughter about her position before God. Has she made a confession of faith? Is she close to understanding how important the baby birth we celebrate at Christmas is to her?

A Verse to Remember

My sheep recognize my voice; I know them, and they follow me. I give them eternal life, and they will never perish.

John 10:27-28

Night Run to Egypt

Matthew 2:1-23

"Whew! I'm tired. Bed is going to feel good tonight," Joseph thought. He punched his pillow into a comfortable position and drifted off to sleep. But, just a few hours later something very strange happened. "Joseph, wake up. I have a message for you. It's from God." The voice interrupted Joseph's sleep, just enough for him to peek open one eye- something brilliant white stood in front of him- an angel . . . and it looked kind of familiar.

"I know you. You came to me when I was sleeping once before and told me that Mary was going to have a baby that was the son of God," Joseph whispered, so he wouldn't wake Mary.

"That's right. I am an angel, sent by God. He wants you to get up right now. Take Mary and little Jesus and get out of town," the angel said.

"But why? We're settled here in Bethlehem. I've got a good carpentry business built up and Mary has made friends," Joseph was confused by the command to leave town.

"King Herod wants to kill Jesus-he is jealous that Jesus is called the King of the Jews. You've got to run . . . now. Take your little family and go to Egypt. I'll tell you when it's safe to come home," the angel said firmly. Then he disappeared.

Joseph jumped up and threw a few things into a bag. "Mary, get up. Get Jesus-we've got to get out of town-fast!" Mary knew better than to argue with Joseph when he used that tone of voice. She didn't even take time to pack a few things. As they disappeared into the darkness, Joseph explained what the angel had told him.

The little family arrived safely in Egypt. It was hard to live there-the people spoke a different language and there was no temple to worship God. "But, Jesus is safe and that's the most important thing," Joseph reminded Mary when she got discouraged.

A few years later, the angel came again, "It's safe to go home now. King Herod is dead." Mary and Joseph happily returned to their home town, Nazareth. It was good to be with family again!

Based on Matthew 2:1-23

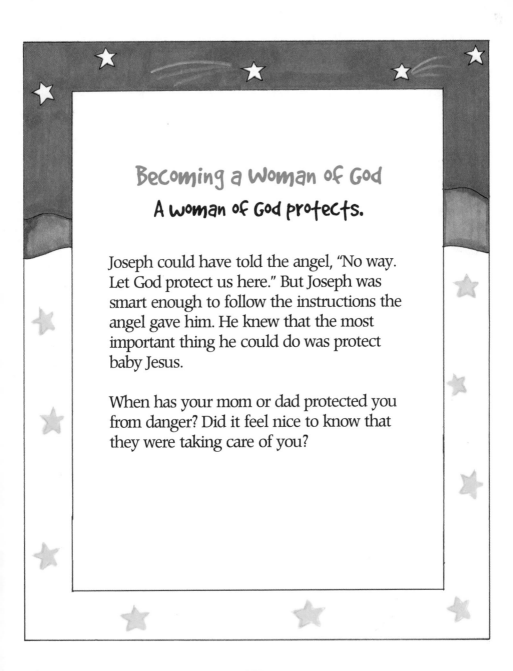

Becoming a Woman of God
A Woman of God protects.

Joseph could have told the angel, "No way. Let God protect us here." But Joseph was smart enough to follow the instructions the angel gave him. He knew that the most important thing he could do was protect baby Jesus.

When has your mom or dad protected you from danger? Did it feel nice to know that they were taking care of you?

Dad's Turn

A big part of parenting is protecting your children from danger or from bad choices they make because they are immature. Tell your daughter about a time you protected her, perhaps she didn't even realize it was happening.

Remind your daughter that the rules you make for her are usually to keep her safe. Talk about some of the rules you have made for her. Explain to her how they are for her safety. Talk about ways God protects us. Thank him for his protection.

A Verse to Remember

The LORD keeps watch over you as you come and go, both now and forever.

Psalm 121:8

The Temptation of Jesus

Jesus was the son of God. Everyone knew it, at least everyone who was at the Jordan River when John the Baptist baptized Jesus. It was hard to miss because a voice boomed from heaven announcing, "This is my Son and I'm very pleased with him."

Not long after his baptism, Jesus left his mom and dad and everyone he knew. He went out to the wilderness all by himself.

"This is my Son and I'm very pleased with him."

For forty days and forty nights Jesus sat alone in the wilderness.
He had no food and nothing to drink. No friends or family to talk
with . . . the only person who came to be with him was his
biggest enemy . . . Satan.

"What's wrong, Jesus? Are you hungry? Ohhh, poor guy, I can hear your stomach growling. Well, here's an idea-you're the son of God, right? Why don't you just turn these stones into bread?" Satan snarled, tossing a handful of stones at Jesus' feet.

"No, the Scriptures say that people need more than bread for life. They need to feed on the Word of God," Jesus answered and turned his back on Satan.

Do not test the Lord

Satan whisked Jesus to the highest point at the top of the temple. "If you're really the Son of God, jump off," he challenged. "Your high falutin' Scriptures say that God will send his angels to keep you from so much as stubbing your toe."

"If you really knew the Scriptures you would know they say not to test the Lord," Jesus answered quietly.

Faster than you can say "Hezekiah", Satan took Jesus to the top of a tall mountain. "Look around you-see all the nations of the world. See their glory and riches? Impressive, isn't it? Well, it can all be yours. Yeah, I can give it to you. All you have to do is bow down and worship me," Satan's voice dropped very low.

"Get outta here," Jesus whispered, "the Scriptures say to worship only God!"

Based on Matthew 4:1-11

Becoming a Woman of God
A woman of God fights temptation.

Jesus knows what it's like for us when we're tempted to do something wrong. He understands the urge to "take care of number one". He understands the temptation to make yourself more important than others. He understands the pull of being rich and famous. Satan hit him with all those-and Jesus answered each one with a verse of Scripture.

Are you ever tempted to feel more important than someone else or to take the biggest piece of cake? How do you fight temptation?

Dad's Turn

Temptation is a part of life, isn't it? Sometimes Satan is sneaky with temptation and we don't even realize what's happening. Tell your daughter about a temptation you struggle with, for example, the temptation to work too many hours and not be with the family more. Or, temptation to be critical of other people. Tell your daughter how you handle temptation.

Jesus answered Satan with Bible verses. Do you memorize Bible verses? When you are feeling tempted, do those verses ever pop into your mind to help you?

A Verse to Remember

Your word is a lamp for my feet and a light for my path.

Psalm 119:105

The Beginning

John 2:1-11

Mary didn't get to see Jesus much anymore since he was grown up. He spent most of his time with his friends. So, she was excited to see him at the same wedding celebration she was invited to. The party after the wedding usually lasted for days. Mary enjoyed seeing old friends and catching up with what was happening in their lives.

"Isn't the bride beautiful?" Mary whispered to a friend. The whole event was wonderful and Mary was happier than she had been in a long time. Then, she heard the master of ceremonies worrying about something. "Oh dear," she thought. "I hate for anything to spoil this special day. I know Jesus can help." Searching through the crowd, she saw Jesus and ran to him. "The party isn't over, but they've run out of wine," she told him.

"I can't help them. It's not time for me to
do miracles yet," Jesus whispered to her.
Mary stared at him with a look that only a
mother can give.

Turning to the servants, she said, "Do
whatever Jesus tells you to do."

He looked at his mother for a long time,
then said, "Fill six big jars with water."

Mary couldn't wait to see what would happen. The servants filled the jars and brought them to Jesus. He didn't even touch them, but just said, "Dip some out and take it to the master of ceremonies."

She wanted to jump up and down in excitement when the man said, "This is the best wine I've ever tasted!" The servants' mouths dropped open-they knew they had put water in those jars-not wine!

Mary looked around for Jesus. She wanted to thank him for helping, but he was nowhere around. Mary knew this was just the first of many miracles he would do. His disciples seemed to be in shock. Now they knew for sure that Jesus wasn't just an ordinary man-he was the Son of God. Mary sighed, "Well, nothing will ever be the same for him now. Soon everyone will know that Jesus is God's own Son."

Based on John 2:1-11

THE WHOLE WORLD WILL KNOW HIM

Becoming a Woman of God
A Woman of God recognizes Jesus' Power.

Mary knew who Jesus was. She believed in his power and expected him to help people who needed his help. She even expected him to do miracles . . . before he had ever done one. Jesus saw how much faith she had and he did his first miracle at this wedding. Many more miracles followed.

It's a good thing to see Jesus' power and to expect him to help you when you need it. That's what faith is. Recognizing Jesus power and expecting him to help you is why you pray to him.

Dad's Turn

Share a story with your daughter of a time when you saw Jesus' power. Perhaps you were made aware of his power through something in nature or through a wonderful answer to prayer.

Did that experience cause you to recognize his power even more and expect answers the next time you prayed?

Encourage your daughter to recognize Jesus' power. Talk about ways you see his power around you. Encourage her to call on that power when she prays and to expect him to answer.

A Verse to Remember

When you ask him, be sure that you really expect him to answer.

James 1:6

Just a Word

Matthew 8:5-13

"Sir. I polished your shield last night," the servant leaned the shiny shield against the wall and saluted.

The Roman officer had to struggle a bit to keep from patting the servant on the back-that just wasn't something an officer did. "Thank you. I appreciate that you are so attentive. You seem to know what I need before I even know."

The servant bowed slightly as he left the room. He was happy to serve the officer the best way he could. The officer was an important man in the Roman army and he had many servants. Not all of them served happily, so he was especially fond of this good servant-in fact, he almost seemed like a son.

A few days later the officer was working at his desk when another servant dashed into the room. "Forgive me for disturbing you, Sir. But one of your servants is sick-very sick!" The officer ran to the servant's quarters and found his special servant lying in bed, moaning and crying for relief from terrible pain.

The Roman officer didn't know what to do to help his servant. He paced around the room, barking orders for pillows to be brought and ice water. But, he knew he was really helpless. Then he remembered hearing that Jesus was in town. "That's the man who heals sick people using the power of God," he remembered. Grabbing his helmet, he ran for town.

"Sir, my servant is very sick. He's a good servant . . . a good person," the officer told Jesus.

"I'll come and heal him," Jesus was already heading for the officer's house.

"That's not necessary. If you just say the word, I know he will be healed. I have servants, I know that when I speak, they carry out my wishes," the officer said.

Jesus couldn't believe what he was hearing, "I haven't seen this kind of faith ever before," he told his followers. "Go on home," he told the officer. "Your servant is well."

Based on Matthew 8:5-13

Becoming a Woman of God
A woman of God helps others.

This Roman officer got quite a compliment from Jesus, didn't he? Jesus said that he had never seen this kind of faith before. The officer didn't think that Jesus had to actually come and touch his servant—he didn't have to come at all. This man had so much faith that he believed Jesus could just say the words and the servant would be healed.

How big is your faith? When you ask God to do something, do you really truly believe that he will do it? Do you pray for other people and believe that God will answer?

Dad's Turn

The first thing we notice about the Roman officer is that he really cared for his servant— and he sought Jesus' help on his servant's behalf. Tell your daughter about a time when you helped someone else. What did you do? How did you help?

Encourage your daughter to trust God more and more. Help her remember the times that God has answered prayers and met her needs. Help her learn to believe that God can handle anything.

A Verse to Remember

I have trusted in the LORD without wavering.

Psalm 26:1

Getting Out of the BOAT

"Man, I'm tired," Peter announced as he settled down in the boat. Just then the boat lurched sideways and he was nearly tossed out. "Andrew, can't you hold this thing a little steadier?" Peter growled.

"Hey, you're welcome to try it yourself. This storm is getting so bad that the water is bouncing us all over," Andrew shouted back.

"Come on, guys, don't waste energy fighting. We all need to help if we're going to keep ourselves out of the water," John shouted over the sound of the wind. Everyone worked to keep the boat level and water out of it.

"I wish Jesus was here," someone said. "Stuff is always okay when he's with us."

"Well, he's not and we're in trouble here!" Peter shouted back. "Get busy!"

For a few minutes all twelve men worked quietly. Then someone said, "Guys, look over there. Do you see something? Is it another boat that's in trouble or what?"

Peter brushed the water from his eyes as he stared through the roaring waves. "It looks more like a man. That's crazy-how could a man be walking around on the water . . . in a storm?"

"It must be a ghost!" Peter suddenly voiced the fear that was in everyone's heart. "God, help us!" he shouted in panic.

"Hey, it's me! Don't be afraid, I'm just coming to help you," a voice called.

"J-J-Jesus???" Peter leaned over the side of the boat to get a better look. "Jesus, is that you? If it is, let me come to you."

It almost sounded like Jesus was laughing when he called, "Okay, come on!"

In a split second Peter was out of the boat and running across the water! "I'm coming, Jesus!" he called. He looked back at the rest of the disciples in the boat. They were looking at Peter like he had lost his head . . . and when he realized that he was walking on water, Peter sank like a lead weight. "H-e-l-p m-e!!!" he cried.

Jesus was by his side in a minute, lifting him into the boat. As Peter coughed water from his lungs, Jesus quietly said, "You don't have much faith, do you, Peter? Didn't you trust me to keep you safe?"

Based on Matthew 14:22-33

Becoming a Woman of God
A woman of God gets out of the boat.

Peter took a chance-without even thinking about it. He wanted to be with Jesus so badly that he hopped right out of the boat when Jesus called him. Peter would have been OK if he had just kept his eyes on Jesus and not looked back at his buddies. For just an instance, Peter showed awesome faith, the kind of faith that can do exciting things for God.

When have you tried doing something new? Was it exciting or were you afraid? Did you try it a second time, too?

Dad's Turn

Tell your daughter about an experience you had when you tried something new. Was it hard? Were you nervous? Did you enjoy it enough to try it again. Did it change your opinions about things?

Ask your daughter to think about something new she might like to try. Then plan out how you can help her to have a new experience.

A Verse to Remember

The LORD is my light and my salvation,
so why should I be afraid?

Psalm 27:1

The king of a great and powerful land decided to call in all the debts that were owed to him. "Bring the books of my kingdom," he commanded a servant. The king carefully looked through the books to see who owed money to the government. One name jumped out at him-a man who owed him millions of dollars! "My treasury will be even more full if this man pays me back," the king thought.

"Pay me back now! Otherwise, you, your wife, and your children will be sold as slaves," the king told the man. The poor man was scared silly. His wife and children stood behind him shaking and crying.

"Please, your highness, have mercy on me. I'll pay it all back, I promise. Just give me some time!" he begged. The king had a soft heart, so he released the family and forgave the debt. The man didn't ever have to pay it back!

The man and his wife danced with joy! "He forgave our debt! We don't have to pay a thing!" they couldn't believe how lucky they were.

As they were walking home, the man saw another man who happened to owe him a few thousand dollars. "Hey you, pay up. I want my money NOW!" he grabbed the man by the collar!

The poor man didn't know what hit him. But, what he did know was that he didn't have any money. "I can't pay-just give me some time and I'll get the money. I promise!"

"Forget it, buddy. You're going to jail!" the angry man shouted. Some of the king's servants saw this whole thing. They knew that the king had forgiven the first man's debt-which was much bigger than the second man's debt.

The servants ran to the king and told him what had happened. He was mad! The king had the first man thrown into jail until he could pay back the millions of dollars he owed the government. "I forgave your big debt. You should have forgiven the other man's debt, too," the king said.

Jesus told this story to teach us about forgiving people because God forgives us.

Based on Matthew 18:23-35

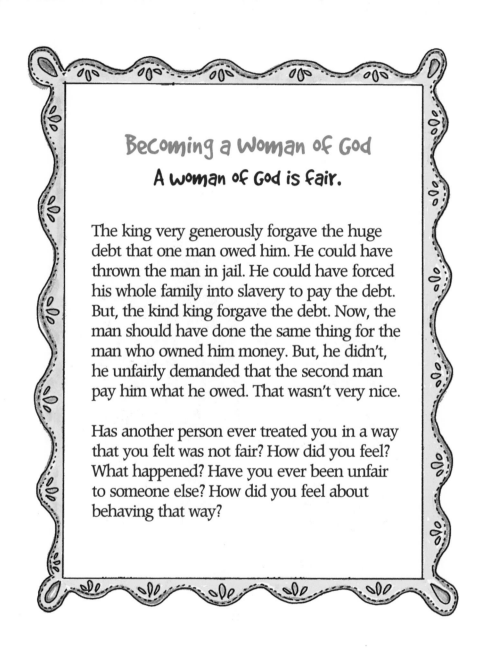

Becoming a Woman of God
A woman of God is fair.

The king very generously forgave the huge debt that one man owed him. He could have thrown the man in jail. He could have forced his whole family into slavery to pay the debt. But, the kind king forgave the debt. Now, the man should have done the same thing for the man who owned him money. But, he didn't, he unfairly demanded that the second man pay him what he owed. That wasn't very nice.

Has another person ever treated you in a way that you felt was not fair? How did you feel? What happened? Have you ever been unfair to someone else? How did you feel about behaving that way?

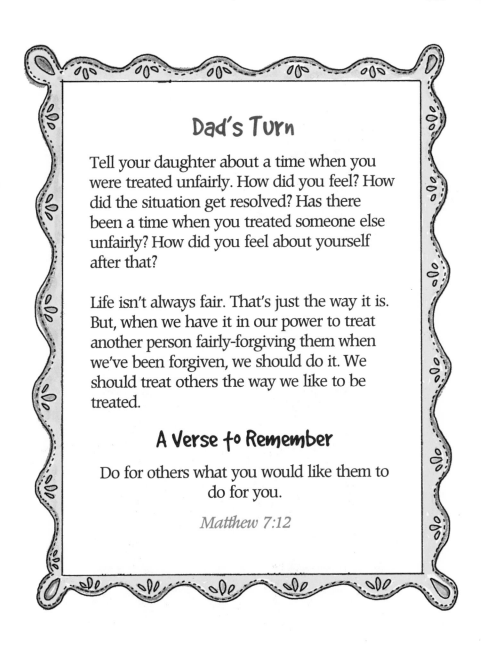

Dad's Turn

Tell your daughter about a time when you were treated unfairly. How did you feel? How did the situation get resolved? Has there been a time when you treated someone else unfairly? How did you feel about yourself after that?

Life isn't always fair. That's just the way it is. But, when we have it in our power to treat another person fairly-forgiving them when we've been forgiven, we should do it. We should treat others the way we like to be treated.

A Verse to Remember

Do for others what you would like them to do for you.

Matthew 7:12

The young man often rode down the street in his fancy carriage with it's gold and jewels shining. The horses that pulled his carriage were the finest that could be found.

He liked it when people stopped to stare at him. "They must think that I am an important person because I have so much money," he thought.

your Money

or Your Life!

Matthew 19:16-24

One day as the rich man was riding through town, he saw a crowd of people sitting under a tree listening to a man teach. "Stop the carriage!" he shouted. He got out and walked over to the crowd. His gold jewelry bangled as he walked and he didn't even try to keep it quiet.

"Shhhh!" someone said. "We're trying to hear what Jesus says!"

"Hmmph," the rich man snorted. "Do you know who I am?" He thought that perhaps the people had somehow missed the fact that he was rich and important.

But no one seemed to care that he was rich or important. The rich man listened to what Jesus was teaching for a few minutes. He was talking about eternal life. "That might be a good thing to have," the rich man thought. When Jesus was finished, the rich man walked right up to him and asked, "What good thing do I have to do to get eternal life?" He jingled the gold in his pocket, thinking that he might be able to buy some eternal life.

Jesus completely ignored the money, "There's only one way-obey the commandments."

"Which ones?" the rich man asked.

Jesus answered, "Don't murder, commit adultery, steal, or lie. Honor your father and mother and love your neighbor as much as you love yourself."

"No problem," said the rich man. I've done all those."

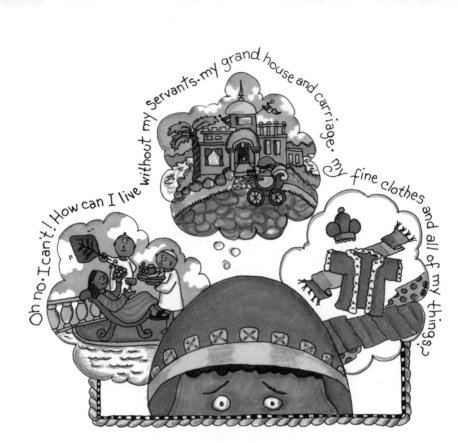

"Then," Jesus continued, "sell everything you own and give the money away to the poor." The rich man was shocked-he couldn't believe Jesus would say such a thing. He thought about his fine house and fancy carriage. He thought about his servants and his beautiful clothes. He thought about the piles of money he owned. The rich man shook his head and walked away-he couldn't do what Jesus asked.

Based on Matthew 19:16-24

Becoming a Woman of God
A woman of God keeps God most important.

The rich man really liked being rich. He wasn't really that interested in having eternal life if it meant that he couldn't be rich and important anymore. He didn't want God to have first place in his life, he wanted to still be in control himself.

What kinds of things are important to you? Is there something that creeps into the place of being more important to you than God? What is it?

Dad's Turn

It's important for your daughter to know that all people struggle with keeping God in first place in their lives at one time or another. Be honest with her as you tell her what kinds of things creep in front of God in your heart. Talk about how you confess that to God and constantly strive to keep him most important to you.

Remind your daughter that keeping the Commandments is important, but the attitude of our hearts are even more important. If we desire to serve God, even though we may sometimes fail to keep him in first place, he will know that is our basic desire.

A Verse to Remember

Love the LORD your God with all your heart, all your soul, and all your strength.

Deuteronomy 6:5

"Chores, chores chores! Why do we have to spend all our time working?" one boy asked, as he finished sweeping the floor.

"Yeah, we're kids. We should be playing games and having fun. There will be plenty of time to work when we're grown up!" his brother answered, putting the last clean plate in the cupboard.

Just then Father came in, "Will you please go pick grapes in the vineyard this afternoon?" he asked his oldest son.

"NO! All I do is work. I'm tired of it," the boy stomped out of the house.

"How about you? Will you help in the vineyards?" Father asked his younger boy.

"I guess so," the boy said. He wasn't excited about it-but he didn't want to argue.

But as he was leaving, the boy's brand new puppy ran up. He started wrestling with the puppy, and forgot all about working in the vineyard.

Later, Father came home, "Son, you said you'd pick grapes for me today, but you didn't do it. Since you didn't do what you said you would do, I'm going to have to work overtime to get the work done." Father wasn't very happy.

Father walked slowly to the vineyard. He was tired and
disappointed with his son. But, when he got to the vineyard, he
saw something that surprised him so much he nearly fainted.

There was his older son working away-picking grapes-the
same work he had angrily said he wouldn't do.

"Thank you, thank you, thank you!" Father shouted. "I am so glad you changed your mind. Your brother said he would help, but he didn't. I thought he was the obedient son today-but it really is you because you are actually doing the work!" Father picked up his basket and began working with his son.

Based on Matthew 21:28-32

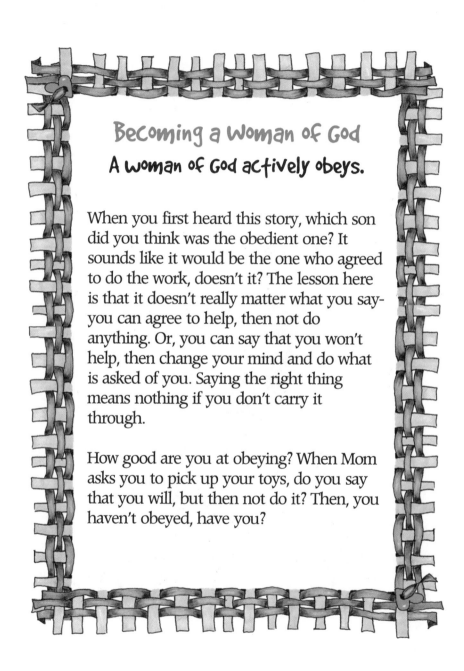

Becoming a Woman of God
A woman of God actively obeys.

When you first heard this story, which son did you think was the obedient one? It sounds like it would be the one who agreed to do the work, doesn't it? The lesson here is that it doesn't really matter what you say- you can agree to help, then not do anything. Or, you can say that you won't help, then change your mind and do what is asked of you. Saying the right thing means nothing if you don't carry it through.

How good are you at obeying? When Mom asks you to pick up your toys, do you say that you will, but then not do it? Then, you haven't obeyed, have you?

Dad's Turn

So, how are you at obeying? Can you share a story with your daughter about how you obeyed your parents? When was a specific time that you didn't obey? What happened? When was a time that you did obey and how did you feel afterwards?

Talk to your daughter about obeying. When you instruct her to do something, she shouldn't say OK just to get you to stop talking about it. Remind her that obeying is only real, when the actual job is done.

A Verse to Remember

Good people are guided by their honesty.

Proverbs 11:3

Ninety-nine and Counting

The gentle thump, thump, thump of sheep hooves on grass broke the silence of the early morning. The shepherd led his flock to a field filled with sweet green grass. While the sheep ate breakfast, he settled down under a tree and kept a sharp eye out for any animals that might think about attacking his flock.

One little runty lamb wandered farther and farther from the herd. "That goofy thing," the shepherd thought. "I'm always shooing him back into the flock. Why can't he stay with the group like the other young lambs do?" But, the shepherd picked up his staff and gently led the lamb back to the flock.

After the sheep finished eating, many of them napped. The shepherd settled back against the tree and closed his eyes, too. The hot sun made him sleepy, but he didn't let himself go to sleep because he had to protect his flock from whatever might happen. They were his first responsibility.

Later in the afternoon the shepherd stood up and stretched. He called his sheep to follow him, using the special call that they would recognize as his. The shepherd climbed up on a big rock and counted each sheep as they passed below him. "One, two, three . . ." He knew every sheep in his flock. "ninety-seven, ninety-eight, ninety-nine . . ." That wasn't right. Where was the 100th sheep? The shepherd jumped down and wandered among the sheep trying to get another count. No, he had been right, there was one missing.

"The one missing is that little runt. Well, that's no surprise, but where could he be?" Without even thinking about it, the shepherd left the ninety-nine sheep alone and ran to find the missing lamb. It didn't matter that he still had ninety-nine sheep. It didn't matter that the missing one was always wandering off by himself. The shepherd searched until he found the little lamb and he brought him safely back to the flock.

Based on Luke 15:1-7

Becoming a Woman of God
A woman of God knows she is special to him.

The shepherd had ninety-nine sheep left. Why did he care if one goofy little sheep wandered away? Why didn't he just let it go? Because every single sheep was important to that shepherd. This story reminds us that every single person is important to God, too. God wants every single person to know him and love him. He goes out of his way to find any person who might be lost.

Have you ever lost something? What was it? Was it special to you? How long did you look for it? Did you find it? How did you feel when you found it?

Dad's Turn

When was a time that you lost something you really cared about? What did you do? Did you just forget about it and not even look? Tell your daughter about losing it and how you felt. Did you ever find it?

Remind your daughter how very important she is to you and that she is even more important to God. Talk about all the things God does for her and gives her . . . including a dad who loves her!

A Verse to Remember

Lead me by your truth and teach me, for you are the God who saves me. All day long I put my hope in you.

Psalm 25:5

The Last Chance

Mark 5:25-34

"I've got nothing to lose. I know he can help me—but if his friends stop me from getting close to him, well, I've got nothing to lose," the woman thought again. She had been sick for a long time—been to every doctor-tried every miracle cure suggested. Nothing helped, she was as sick today as at the very beginning. The problem was Jesus was always surrounded by crowds of people, begging him to do things for them.

I Know He can help me.

The woman took a deep breath and pushed her way through the crowd of people behind Jesus. Bending down low, she quietly touched the hem of his robe. Her faith in him was so strong that she believed this simple touch could heal her. As her fingers brushed the fabric, she felt something shoot through her body. "Unnhh," she grunted and fell to the ground as the crowd kept moving.

The woman was still trying to figure out what had happened to her when she heard Jesus ask, "Who touched me?" His disciples tried to brush off his question-after all, people were pushing against him on every side. Dozens of people touched him every hour.

But Jesus asked again, "Who touched me?" The woman felt like he was looking right at her even though she was hidden behind the crowd of people. "Someone touched me-I felt power leave me," Jesus said again.

She wanted to turn and run. No one ever had to know what she had done . . . but she couldn't do that. "I touched you. It was me," she said softly. The crowd parted like the Red Sea until she was standing face to face with Jesus. "I've been sick so long. I just wanted to be well and I knew that touching you would heal me," she whispered, not daring to look up.

Everyone was quiet, waiting to hear what Jesus would say. But, he waited for the woman to continue. "When I touched your robe, I felt something. I think I'm well." A ripple of shock rolled through the crowd.

Jesus smiled gently before saying, "It was your faith that made you well. Go live your life in peace."

Based on Mark 5:25-34

Becoming a Woman of God
A woman of God takes a chance.

This woman had been sick a long time, she had tried everything she could think of to get well. Nothing worked. She believed that Jesus could help her. In fact, she had such strong faith that she believed just touching his clothing, and not even bothering him would help her. She didn't think he needed to touch her or even speak to her to touch her. She also knew that she was taking a chance by reaching through the crowd to touch him. But, it meant that much to her to get well.

Faith means that you believe something is true even if you can't actually see it. That kind of belief gives you the strength to take a chance. For this woman, taking a chance meant she was healed!

Dad's Turn

Sometimes taking a chance means something like trying skydiving or riding in a hot air balloon. When have you taken a chance like that? Tell your daughter about the courage it took to do that.

Encourage your daughter to take a chance by trying something new and trusting God to help her accomplish it. Encourage her to be brave and courageous.

A Verse to Remember

This same God who takes care of me will supply all your needs from his glorious riches which have been given to us in Christ Jesus.

Philippians 4:19

A Miracle Touch

"Where's my girl?" The little girl ran to her dad and he lifted her high in the air. She adored her daddy and believed that he could do anything. As far as she was concerned, her daddy was the smartest, strongest, bravest and kindest daddy who ever lived. Then something terrible happened-the little girl got very, very sick. For the first time in her life, something happened that her daddy couldn't automatically fix.

Mark 5:22-24, 35-43

God Bless You

I ♥ LOVE YOU ♥
DADDY

"Don't worry, baby," Daddy whispered, kissing her goodbye. "I'm going to find someone who can help you. Just hang on, I'll be back soon." Jairus had heard about a man named Jesus-a man who healed sick people in God's name. He was determined to get Jesus to help his precious daughter-money was no object. The little girl trusted her daddy. He always did what he said he would do.

The little girl laid back in her bed and rested. She believed her daddy would be back soon with Jesus. She waited and waited, getting weaker every day. Her momma stayed with her and prayed every day for her daughter to get better. The little girl tried to hang on. She thought about her dad every day, but she kept getting weaker and weaker. Before her daddy could come back, the little girl died.

The heartbroken mother sent a servant to tell her husband not to bother Jesus. "Your little girl is dead," the servant whispered gently. "Don't bother Jesus anymore." Sadly, Jairus turned to go home. Then, he felt a hand on his arm. "I'm coming with you," Jesus said.

Jesus went right to the little girl's room. "Why are you crying?" he asked. "She's not dead, just sleeping." When people laughed at him, Jesus sent them all away-except Jairus and his wife. Then he took the little girl's hand and said, "Get up, little girl." AND SHE DID!

Now Jairus knew that Jesus healed sick people and brought dead people back to life by the power of God. For the rest of his life, Jairus reminded his daughter of the special miracle that gave her back to him.

Based on Mark 5:22-24, 35-43

Becoming a Woman of God
A Woman of God thanks God for second chances.

Jairus' daughter got a second chance at life. Don't you think she felt special when her dad told her the story of Jesus bringing her back to life over and over? She knew that her dad loved her and Jesus loved her. And she had a second chance to live a long life and live her life for God.

Have you ever gotten a second chance at something? Maybe a time when you disobeyed and Mom or Dad gave you another chance. Or maybe you didn't do well on a test at school and the teacher gave you another chance to take the test.

Dad's Turn

Life is filled with second chances. A wise person makes the most of those chances and tries to do better the second time. Tell your daughter about a time when you were given a second chance. Did you take the second chance seriously and do a better job that time? How did you feel about the person who gave you that second chance?

Ask your daughter how she feels when you give her a second chance to obey or explain her actions to you. Remind her that God gives us second and third and fourth (and on and on) chances to obey when we confess our sins and ask his forgiveness.

A Verse to Remember

I confessed all my sins to you and stopped trying to hide them. And you forgave me!

Psalm 32:5

Giving From the ♥ Heart

Mark 12:41-44

The old woman loved to come to the temple. She loved God and especially loved to watch people giving their offerings to him and worshipping as they prayed. "This is a holy place," she always thought. She peeked out from behind a pillar, waiting for her turn to give. "Praise you, God," she prayed. "Thank you for everything you have given me. You are so good!"

If anyone heard her prayer, they would have laughed right out loud. The woman was so poor that she never knew where her next meal was coming from. Her husband was dead and she didn't have much family left. But, she loved God and always praised him.

Stepping into line, the woman held her little bag with two small coins tightly in her hand and waited for her turn.

A very important man stepped up to the offering box ahead of her. He made a big show of dropping gold coins in the box as he loudly prayed, "O God, I am so important and so rich. You are very lucky to have a man like me paying attention to you!" The rich man made sure that everyone in the temple noticed how important and how generous he was.

When it was her turn, the old widow stepped up to the box
and opened her little bag. She took out the two small coins and
dropped them into the offering box. They didn't make much
noise-together they were barely worth a penny, but her heart
was filled with praise to God. The rich man who had been
ahead of her exploded in laughter, "That offering isn't even
worth the space it takes up in the box."

The old woman didn't hear him though, she was busy praying that God would use her offering to help people who were poorer than she was. Struggling to her feet, the woman glanced across the temple and her eyes met Jesus. He knew that this poor woman had given everything she had to God's work, while the rich men only gave their extra money to God. Jesus smiled and her heart filled with praise.

Based on Mark 12:41-44

Becoming a Woman of God
A woman of God is humble.

This woman didn't hold anything back from God. Her heart belonged to God and she wanted to give everything to him. She was also very humble. She didn't care if people noticed her in the temple, giving to God. The rich man ahead of her was more concerned with the show of giving and having everyone know how important he was.

Do you know anyone who is always bragging about how smart they are or how good they are at something? Do you enjoy being around a person like that? Probably not, most people don't enjoy hearing others brag.

Dad's Turn

Tell your daughter about a humble person you have known. Point out that a humble person doesn't have to own the best of everything, but is happy with what he has. Usually a humble person is happy when someone else succeeds or does well.

Encourage your daughter to give part of her allowance to God's work. Help her to see how giving to God's work is important.

A Verse to Remember

Don't be selfish; don't live to make a good impression on others. Be humble, thinking of others as better than yourself.

Philippians 2:3

A Surprise Friend

BASED ON LUKE 10:30-37

"Honey, I'm going," a man called as he stuffed a bag of coins into his pocket.

"OK, be careful," his wife answered from the backyard where she was hanging out laundry. The man set out on his weekly walk to Jericho to do business.

He was enjoying his walk, until two men jumped him from behind. They hit him and kicked him until he dropped to the ground. They must have thought he was dead, so they took his money and shoes . . . even his clothes.

"Ohhh," the man moaned. "I hurt all over. Who's going to help me here on this empty road?" He thought for sure he would die there. But, then he heard footsteps. It took all of his energy to lift his head to see who was coming. "Oh thank the Lord, it's a priest! If anyone will stop to help me, a priest will." But, the priest curled up his nose and said right out loud, "What is this mess doing in my way?" He crossed the road and kept right on walking.

What is this mess....

The sun was straight overhead now and the poor man was hot and thirsty. "Maybe I'm dreaming, but I think I hear footsteps again," he thought, straining to see who was coming. "Thank goodness, a temple worker. Help me, please!" all he could manage was a whisper.

"Wow, you're in pretty bad shape," the temple worker said, "but, I've got to get to work-sorry," he stepped right over the man and kept on walking.

It was nearly dark before the man heard someone else passing by. This time he didn't open his eyes or make a sound. He had given up on anyone helping him. But then, he felt someone gently lift his head and slide a pillow underneath. "This has to be a dream," he thought as he peeked through one eye. "This fellow is a Samaritan-they hate us Jews. Why would he stop to help me?"

The poor man must have passed out then. But, he woke up later in a nice clean bed. His cuts were clean and bandaged. The Samaritan was asking the innkeeper to take care of the hurt man- he even paid him gold pieces for the man's room and care. "Well, you never know who your friends really are . . . until you need them," he thought as he snuggled in to go back to sleep.

Based on Luke 10:30-37

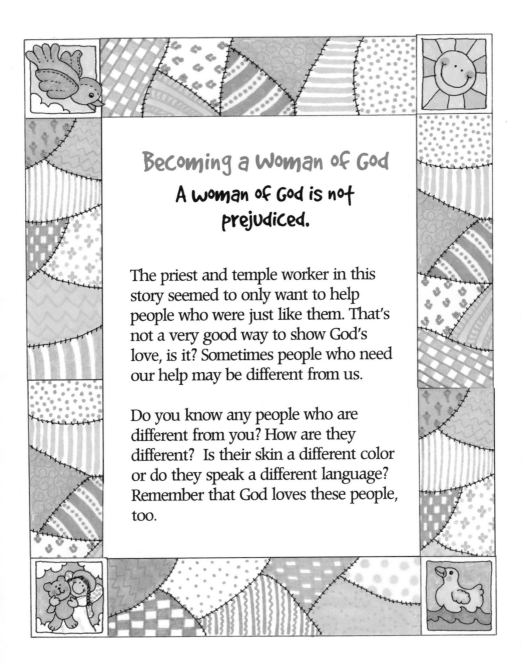

Becoming a Woman of God
A Woman of God is not prejudiced.

The priest and temple worker in this story seemed to only want to help people who were just like them. That's not a very good way to show God's love, is it? Sometimes people who need our help may be different from us.

Do you know any people who are different from you? How are they different? Is their skin a different color or do they speak a different language? Remember that God loves these people, too.

Dad's Turn

Explain what prejudice is to your daughter. Do you have a story about becoming friends with someone who is different from you? Share it with her.

Encourage your daughter to get to know people of other cultures and other races. Talk about how God loves all people and Jesus died for everyone.

A Verse to Remember

Love each other. Just as I have loved you, you should love each other.

John 13:34

What's Most Important?

Luke 10:38-42

"Mary, can you at least set the table?" Martha asked in frustration. The sisters had heard a few days ago that Jesus was coming to visit. Ever since then, Martha had cleaned, and dusted, and baked. Everything had to be perfect! That's just the way Martha was-had been her whole life.

Mary and Martha were as different as two sisters could be. Martha was a "doer" and Mary was a "dreamer". Mary loved long walks in the fields, smelling flowers, and just sitting for hours talking to people. Martha was always busy, working in the house or the yard. She couldn't sit still if she saw something that needed to be done-and she always saw something that needed to be done.

Today, Martha chopped and cooked and baked. She wanted to serve Jesus a wonderful dinner. "But," she thought, "it sure would be nice to get an hour of help from Mary."

When Jesus came in, Mary settled down at his feet to listen to his wonderful stories. Martha listened for a few minutes, but then hurried to the kitchen to finish dinner. She thought that Mary would surely come help her in a few minutes. She didn't.

Martha rushed around the kitchen, mixing and stirring. Every few minutes she peeked out to see if Mary was coming yet. She wasn't. In fact, every time Martha looked, Mary and Jesus seemed to be having more fun that the last time. Pretty soon, Martha had all she could take. "Why do I always have to do all the work around here?" she thought, slamming pans onto the table and stirring the soup a little harder than it really needed to be stirred.

Marching into the other room, Martha nearly shouted, "Tell her to get up and help me. I'd like to hear your stories, too, but someone has to make dinner!"

Jesus was surprised at Martha's anger and Mary didn't seem to know what to think. Jesus put his hand on her shoulder and gently said, "Martha, Martha, you work so hard. I really appreciate it, but, I'd rather eat cheese and crackers and have time to talk to you."

Based on Luke 10:38-42

Becoming a Woman of God
A woman of God wants to spend time with Jesus.

Martha meant well. She just wanted to have a nice house and good food to serve her guests. She wanted people to be comfortable when they were her guests. The problem was that she got her priorities mixed up-her housework became more important than the people she was serving-in this story that person was Jesus.

Nothing should be more important than spending time with Jesus. Nothing should get in the way of getting to know Jesus better.

Dad's Turn

Do you ever get so busy doing stuff-even good stuff that you don't have time to spend with people? It's hard to keep the important things of life in the important positions. Sometimes we get busy doing good things-but those things keep us too busy. Talk with your daughter about how hard this is. Ask her if she thinks you spend enough time with her.

Talk about ways to make more time for people. Help your daughter plan a daily schedule that includes quiet time with God. Do that for yourself, too!

A Verse to Remember

I will praise the LORD at all times. I will constantly speak his praises.

Psalm 34:1

"Plant the seed . . . hoe the field . . . mend the fences. I can't take it anymore!" the young man threw the hoe down in disgust. "There must be more to life than this. I want to see the big city- live a little!"

The young man ran into the barn shouting, "Hey Dad, give me my share of your money now. I'm going to get it someday anyway." When his son took the money and headed for the big city, the old man watched sadly.

In the city, the young man was always surrounded by friends who enjoyed helping him spend his money. He loved the fancy clothes and expensive restaurants. But then, he ran out of money ... and suddenly all his "friends" were gone. The boy was all by himself. Meanwhile, his dad kept watching for him to come home.

"I can't believe that none of my friends would help me. I paid for everything for them-before my money ran out. Now, the only job I can get is feeding these pigs and they have more to eat than I do." Meanwhile, his dad kept watching for him to come home.

As the young man walked home, he came up with a plan. "I'll just ask Dad for a job because I don't deserve to be called his son anymore." When his dad ran out to meet him, he tried to say how sorry he was and that he didn't deserve to be called his son anymore, but his dad hugged him so tight that he couldn't get the words out. What the boy didn't know was that his father had watched and watched for him to come home-never giving up hope!

Based on Luke 15:11-32

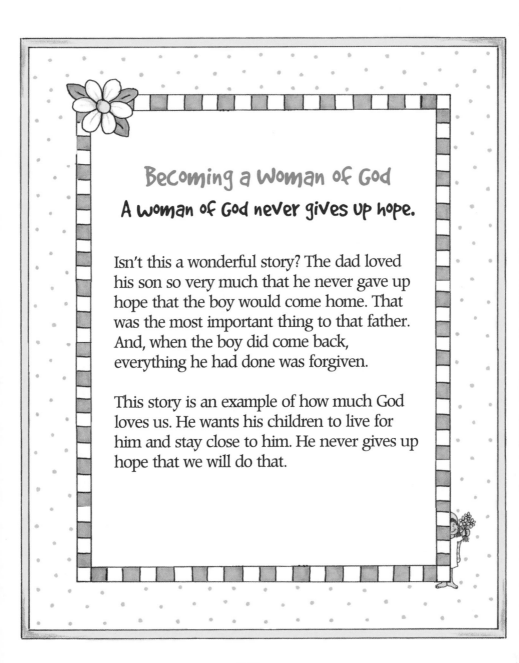

Becoming a Woman of God
A woman of God never gives up hope.

Isn't this a wonderful story? The dad loved his son so very much that he never gave up hope that the boy would come home. That was the most important thing to that father. And, when the boy did come back, everything he had done was forgiven.

This story is an example of how much God loves us. He wants his children to live for him and stay close to him. He never gives up hope that we will do that.

Dad's Turn

Share a story with your daughter about a time when you rebelled against your parents. How did they handle it? Did they ever give up hope that you would come back to them? How did you feel when everything worked out and they welcomed you with open arms?

Tell your daughter how much you love her. Assure her that nothing can ever change that love. Remind her of how much God loves her and that he is always waiting for her to come to him.

A Verse to Remember

Love never gives up.

1 Corinthians 13:7

forgotten Thanks

LUKE 17:11-19

"I hate this rotten disease! Having leprosy means I can't even see my family and I lost my job. I have to live in this lousy leper colony. This stinks!" a man shouted, shaking his fist at the sky.

"I know," another man said quietly. "I wish I could just hug my kids."

Jesus and the crowd of people who were always with him, passed by the leper colony on their way to Jerusalem. "Jesus, please help us!" someone cried. Jesus looked around and saw ten men standing behind some trees. Their heads and hands were wrapped in strips of cloth-they were lepers. The only part of their faces he could see were their eyes. Eyes filled with hope.

Jesus calmly walked toward the men-even though other people were backing away from the lepers. "Go into town and show yourself to the priest," he told them.

People in the crowd whispered, "Did you hear that? He told them to go into town-they can't go near people-they're lepers! Someone might catch the disease from them!"

The ten men took off running toward the nearby town. They didn't care what anyone thought, except Jesus! "Hey, you guys, look at my hands. The white leprosy spots are fading!" one man called to the others.

All ten men stopped and checked their own hands, arms, and faces—anywhere leprosy had been eating away their skin! "It's gone! My leprosy is gone, too! Jesus healed me! I can go home!" each man shouted.

Nine men took off running for their homes and their families. But, one man didn't even hesitate-he turned right around and went back to Jesus. He dropped to the ground, his face near Jesus' feet. "Thank you, thank you so much for healing me," he whispered through his tears.

"You're welcome," Jesus answered, lifting the man to his feet, "but where are the other nine? Didn't I heal ten men???"

Based on Luke 17:11-19

Becoming a Woman of God
A woman of God says thank you.

Jesus healed ten lepers, but only nine took the time to say thank you. How do you think that made Jesus feel? When a person does something really nice for someone else, it's nice to hear a thank you. It makes a person know that what they have done is appreciated.

If a person doesn't remember to say thank you, then people won't want to do nice things for him anymore. Saying "thank you" shows that you know the person made an effort to do something nice for you.

Do you remember to say thank you when someone does something for you? How do you feel when you do something for another person and they don't thank you?

Dad's Turn

Saying thank you is just a nice thing to remember to do. Tell your daughter about a time when someone did a very nice thing for you. Did you remember to thank them? Can you recall a time when you helped someone, and they thanked you? How did you feel? Did you want to do something for that person again?

Make a list together of things God has done for you. Thank him together. Try to remember to thank him for one thing every day.

A Verse to Remember

Give thanks to the LORD and proclaim his greatness. Let the whole world know what he has done.

1 Chronicles 16:8

"How long are you going to let that guy cheat you?" the woman looked helpless as her mean landlord walked away, counting the money he had just cheated her out of.

"Well?" her neighbor asked again.

"I don't know what to do," she said softly.

"Well, if you don't do something, all the money your dead husband left you will be gone. You've got to stop him," the neighbor said.

She knew that her friend was right. The only thing she could think to do was to see the local judge. He might help her . . . though she had heard that he wasn't a very nice man.
"Get outta my sight. Get lost! You're a bunch of losers who can't settle your own family problems!" this judge had forgotten that he was supposed to help people. Most people wondered why he became a judge-he didn't even seem to like people.

"Gulp" the woman took a deep breath before marching up to the judge. "Will you please stop my landlord from cheating me? I'm a widow and I don't have much money," she explained. The judge turned his dark, angry eyes on her and stared for a few minutes.

"Get out of here. I can't be bothered with such piddly problems," he growled.

Sadly turning to leave, the woman was ready to give up easily. "Wait a minute, what do I have to lose?" she thought. "If he doesn't help me I'm going to lose everything anyway." So she marched right back to the judge, "Sir, you are the only one who can help me. Please listen to my story." She almost fainted when the judge shouted, "I said to get out of here!"

But the little woman was not one to give up easily. Time after time she went back to the judge and respectfully asked him to help her with her problem. Time after time, he sent her away. But, every time he looked up, there she was again. Finally he sighed, "You're wearing me out. I'm going to see that you get the help you need because you just keep asking me."

Based on Luke 18:1-8

Becoming a Woman of God
A Woman of God is persistent in prayer.

The little lady could have just asked the judge for help one time, then given up. The judge wasn't very nice, so it was probably hard for her to keep going back to him. But, what she wanted was important to her, so she kept asking and kept asking. Finally, the judge got tired of her bothering him, so he gave her what she wanted.

When you want something from your mom or dad, do you just ask once then give up? If it is something you really want, you ask over and over again, don't you? Sometimes that works and you get what you want, and sometimes it doesn't. But, when you keep asking your parents know that it is important to you.

Dad's Turn

Tell your daughter about something you really wanted when you were a young boy. Explain to her how you asked your parents repeatedly for that thing. Did you finally get it or did you eventually give up?

The Bible tells us to keep asking God when we want him to do something for us. Ask over and over again and don't give up. We won't talk him into doing something he doesn't want to do, but he will know how important that thing is to us.

A Verse to Remember

Keep on asking, and you will be given what you ask for. Keep on looking, and you will find. Keep on knocking, and the door will be opened.

Matthew 7:7

ACTS 3:1-10

"Outta my way, Scum-I said MOVE IT! Don't you know who I am? Let me through . . . I order you to get outta the way!" For once in his life, no one paid any attention to the tough little man.

311

Crowds of people swarmed the streets, and a tax collector, like
Zacchaeus, who cheated and overcharged people had no chance
of anyone letting him move to the front. Everyone wanted to see
Jesus. The famous teacher taught about God, healed sick people,
and raised the dead back to life.

Meanwhile, little Zacchaeus had an idea. A big sycamore
tree grew back off the road a bit. One of it's branches hung
out over the crowd of people. So, Zacchaeus shinnied up the
tree and scooted out to the end of the branch. Now, he was
hanging right over the road where Jesus would pass.

A few minutes later Jesus and a crowd of people appeared down the road. As they moved toward the crowd around the tree, cries of "Jesus, look at me." "Jesus, over here. Heal my friend . . . come to my house," filled the air. Zacchaeus just sat quietly on his tree branch and watched the whole thing.

As Jesus passed under the tree branch, he looked up at Zacchaeus, "Come on down, Zacchaeus. I want to come to your house today."

"Why would Jesus go to a tax collector's house?" people wondered.

But, after Zacchaeus talked with Jesus for a while, he knew it had been wrong to cheat people. The little tax collector promised Jesus to pay back everyone he had cheated-four times more than he had cheated them!

Based on Luke 19:1-10

Becoming a Woman of God
A woman of God changes when she meets Jesus.

Zacchaeus wasn't a nice person. He cheated others and he thought he was more important that the regular people. So, he didn't have many friends and no one wanted to help him when he needed help. He must have been pretty lonely. But, when Jesus talked to him and told him about God's love, Zacchaeus changed. He was sorry for the way he had cheated people and he wanted to change. That must have been hard for people to believe, but that is the effect Jesus had on people.

Have you ever treated someone badly? When you think about how Jesus wants you to treat others are you sorry for being mean or unfair to someone else?

Dad's Turn

Tell your daughter about some change in your life. Did you have a bad habit that you worked to overcome? Did your lifestyle change when you met Jesus? Talk about how it is important to live your life as a good example of who Jesus is.

Remind your daughter that some people may not go to church, but if they know that we are Christians, they will watch how we treat others and decide what God's love is like by how we live.

Ask your daughter if she thinks she needs to make any changes in the way she treats others.

A Verse to Remember

For God so loved the world that he gave his only Son, so that everyone who believes in him will not perish but have eternal life.

John 3:16

My Son, My Savior

John 19:1~30

Mary knew what the Scripture taught about the Messiah. He would save people from their sins. He would be the King of the Jews. She remembered when the angel had come to tell her that she was going to have a baby-God's Son, the Messiah. It was all so confusing now. She had watched Jesus grow into a strong young man. She saw him do miracles-healing the sick, bringing the dead back to life—all the time telling people how much God loved them.

But now, Jesus was going to die and Mary didn't understand why. What had he ever done to hurt anyone? She stood in the crowd watching Jesus struggle down the street, dragging the wooden cross on which he would die. "NO!" she wanted to scream at the soldiers, "you can't do this! He's my son and I love him . . . he's God's Son. Please, someone stop this!" But, she couldn't say a word and no one else did either.

She followed Jesus to a place called Golgotha.
When the soldiers nailed his hands and feet to
the cross, Mary turned away. She couldn't bear
to watch. She wanted to run away-get as far
away from this horrible scene as possible, but
she couldn't. He was her son. She had to stay.

The soldiers dropped the cross into the ground and Mary crept up close to it. Blood and sweat mixed together and ran down Jesus' face. Some of it dripped into little puddles on the ground. Mary looked into his eyes-eyes filled with love, even for those who had done this horrible thing to him.

Mary wished she could roll back time—could warn him against being so open with his miracles and teaching. She would do almost anything to change this horrible ending to Jesus' life.

When Jesus died, Mary dropped to her knees, sobbing in pain, "My son. They've killed my son." But even as she cried, God quietly spoke to her heart, "They've killed MY son," he seemed to say, "and he died to save you from your sins."

Based on John 19:1-30

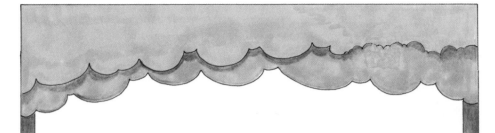

Becoming a Woman of God

A woman of God understands Jesus' sacrifice.

The day that Jesus died was a terrible day for his friends and especially for his mother. They all loved him very much. They knew he had never done anything wrong-no other person has ever been able to say they haven't done one single thing wrong. The truth is that Jesus could have called thousands of angels to rescue him from the cross. But he didn't he died so that we could someday live in heaven with him. He was our sacrifice.

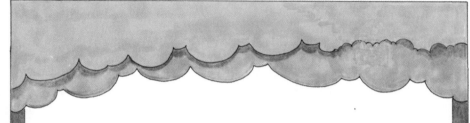

Dad's Turn

Explain what a sacrifice is to your daughter. Tell her that in the Old Testament, before Jesus lived, a lamb was sacrificed to God so the people could ask forgiveness of their sins. Since Jesus died as our sacrifice we don't have to give an animal anymore. He took the blame for our sins.

Have you ever been blamed for something you didn't do? Did you just let it pass or did you argue that you were innocent? Jesus didn't argue . . . he loves us too much. Thank him for his sacrifice.

A Verse to Remember

Believe on the Lord Jesus and you will be saved.

Acts 16:31

A New Beginging

Early Sunday morning, three women silently met up on a small garden path. Without saying much to each other, they headed to the tomb of their friend, Jesus. "I thought he was the King of the Jews," one woman sighed. "I can't believe he's dead . . . murdered."

All three wondered why Jesus didn't call an army of angels to stop his murder. Why did he just let it happen?

How can we move it?

Even in the middle of their pain and confusion, the women wanted to do what was right. That's why they carried baskets filled with spices and perfumes. Their custom was to put these on the bodies of those who had died. They couldn't do it the day Jesus died, because the Sabbath came and no work was permitted. So, they agreed to meet early on Sunday morning and go to the tomb.

"What about the stone?" one woman suddenly asked. The other two stopped so quickly that they nearly spilled the spices from their baskets. "How are we going to move that huge stone in front of the tomb? It took several men just to roll it in place."

One woman began to cry. "This is too much-we've had too much to handle in the last few days!"

"Calm down," the first woman said. "We'll figure something out."

As they rounded the last bend before the tomb, one woman shouted, "It's gone! The stone is gone!" As all three women stared at the open tomb, trying to figure out what this meant an angel stepped through the door. "I know you're looking for Jesus," the angel said. "He isn't here. He came back to life, just as he said he would. Run to town and tell his friends."

For just a moment the women seemed unable to move-unable to believe what had happened. Then they exploded in joy. "He's alive! Jesus is alive!" Jumping and shouting the three women ran to tell the rest of Jesus' friends. "He's alive! Our Savior is alive!"

Based on Luke 24:1-12

Becoming a Woman of God
A Woman of God Celebrates!

The women must have been heartbroken when Jesus died. All their hope died with him. They were probably confused and very very sad. So, when they saw the open tomb and the angel said Jesus was alive, their hearts must have leaped into their throats. They went from being very sad to very, very happy!

What is the absolute happiest you have ever been? What made you so happy? How did you celebrate?

Dad's Turn

Have you ever felt disappointed or hopeless? Tell your daughter what caused that emotion. How did you handle it? What got you over it? What is the happiest you have ever been? How did you celebrate?

Talk with your daughter about what Jesus' resurrection means for us. He overcame death and because of that we have the hope of doing the same-living with him in heaven some day. Celebrate Jesus' resurrection together.

A Verse to Remember

O Lord, you alone are my hope. I've trusted you, O LORD, from childhood.

Psalm 71:5

 WHAT COULD BE BETTER than MONEY?

ACTS 3:1-10

"Come on John, it's almost 3:00. The prayer service will be starting soon." John gulped down the rest of his lunch and wiped his mouth with his hand as he followed Peter out the door. The temple wasn't far away, but the streets were crowded with people.

"Excuse us, coming through!" Some men were trying to get through the crowd. They were carrying a man who couldn't walk.

"They bring that guy here every day to beg for money," Peter observed. He and John watched as the man settled down near the temple gate and started begging from anyone entering the temple.

Peter slowly walked over to the crippled man and just stood in front of him. The man held up his cup, expecting Peter to drop some money in it. "I don't have any money," Peter said quietly.

"Then get out of the way," the man said in disgust. He turned to catch other people going through the gate.

"Look at me," Peter quietly ordered. "I have something better for you than money." The man didn't look so sure-what could be better than money?

"Come on, we're going to be late for prayers," John tugged at Peter's sleeve, but Peter shook him away and turned back to the man.

"In the name of Jesus, GET UP AND WALK," he said.

Peter took the man's hand and helped him to his feet. At first the man didn't understand what had happened-his feet and legs were healed! Carefully trying his new legs, he took at step, then a hop, finally he was jumping and shouting, "I'm healed! I'm healed! Praise God for the gift that is better than money!"

Based on Acts 3:1-10

Becoming a Woman of God
A woman of God gives the best gifts.

The crippled man thought that the best gift he could get was money. But, Peter knew better. He knew that God would help him heal the man. He was willing to interrupt his schedule, be late for the prayer service, in order to help the crippled man.

Have you ever been able to help someone? How did it feel to help someone else? Did it interrupt your schedule or what you were doing? Did you mind?

Dad's Turn

What is the best gift you ever received? Why was it so special? Who gave it to you? What's the best gift you've ever given your daughter? Why did you enjoy giving it so much? Did you ever feel like your schedule was being interrupted in order to give this gift?

Talk about the best gift God has given-salvation through believing in Jesus Christ. Aren't you glad that Jesus didn't worry about his schedule being interrupted? Thank him for his gift of love.

A Verse to Remember

The free gift of God is eternal life through Jesus Christ our Lord.

Romans 6:23

Yours, Mine and Ours

"Why do we always have to meet secretly? Why can't we just sit outside and sing praise to God like we used to?" a young man wondered out loud. Life had not been easy since Jesus was murdered. Some people thought the Christians had stolen his body so it would look like he came back to life. Some people made life really hard for the Christians.

"Don't get discouraged. It's important for us to hang together. We all miss Jesus. We're all confused about what has happened. But, we have to stick together," the disciples stepped up to be leaders of the group of Christians after Jesus left.

"Well, that's easy for you to say. Since I lost my job, my kids are hungry," the young man was really worried. "I'm sorry, I know that God will take care of us. It's just hard sometimes," he whispered.

Barnabas stepped up to the young man and put his arms around the man. "The most important thing for us to do is tell others about Jesus' love. We must be able to tell people that Jesus died because he loves them and that he came back to life and lives in heaven today. You can't do that if you're hungry or worried. Here, I sold some of my land and I want you to have this money."

"I have extra flour and oil," one old woman said. "If anyone needs some to make bread for your family, come see me."

Another man mentioned that he had cows who gave good milk. A young woman had chickens who laid lots of eggs. Everyone started looking for ways they could help one another.

No one in the little church went hungry or had unpaid bills. If one person needed money, someone else sold a field and donated the money. If someone needed help, people volunteered to do what they could. All the time, the Christians shared God's love with others. People in the town could see how much they cared for each other. The Christians were good examples of God's love.

Based on Acts 4:32-37

Becoming a Woman of God
A woman of God shares.

The Christians in this early church took care of one another. If one was hungry or didn't have clothes or a place to live, another man sold some land and gave the money to his needy friend. That's the way we should help one another today.

If you have two blankets and someone else doesn't have any, should you put your extra blanket in a closet, or give it to the other person? Has another person shared something with you? Have you been able to share with another person?

Dad's Turn

Tell your daughter about a time when someone shared something with you. How did you feel about it? How did you feel about that person? Now tell her about a time when you shared with someone. Did you feel good about it? Did the person appreciate what you shared?

Talk about ways you can share what you have with those who are less fortunate. Come up with a plan to work in an inner city neighborhood, or support a child overseas, or give your old clothing to a mission. Find some way you and your daughter can share together.

A Verse to Remember

Blessed are those who are generous.

Proverbs 22:9

Singin', Shakin' and Savin'

"Toss 'em in jail and throw away the key!" "Yeah, the bums are just troublemakers!" Before Paul and Silas could answer sticks were ripping through the air, hitting them and pounding them until they could barely stand. Then they were dragged away to prison.

"You won't escape from here," the jailer pushed Paul and Silas to the floor in the smallest cell, tucked away in the very center of the jail. No windows-no chance to even see daylight or breath fresh air-and no chance for escape or rescue! He roughly clamped their feet into stocks. "You can rot here for all I care," he spat at them.

God will help you...

As soon as they could breathe normally, Paul and Silas started praying and singing praises to God. "What you got to sing about–haven't you noticed that you're in prison or that you've been beaten bloody?" the other prisoners made fun of Paul and Silas.

By midnight, the other prisoners seemed to be comforted by Paul and Silas' singing. They were quiet, listening to the gentle praises. It was about midnight when the floor began to shake. Pieces of the ceiling cracked and dropped down on the prisoners. As the doors broke off and chains popped like paper, men shouted, "We're free! Run!"

But Paul didn't let anyone leave. When the jailer ran in and saw the doors were broken off, he cried, "My prisoners-they've all escaped." He drew his sword to kill himself.

"Stop! We're all here," Paul shouted. The jailer couldn't believe that Paul had kept all the prisoners in the jail.
"Can you tell me how to be a Christian like you?" he asked. Paul was very happy to do just that!

Based on Acts 16:16-34

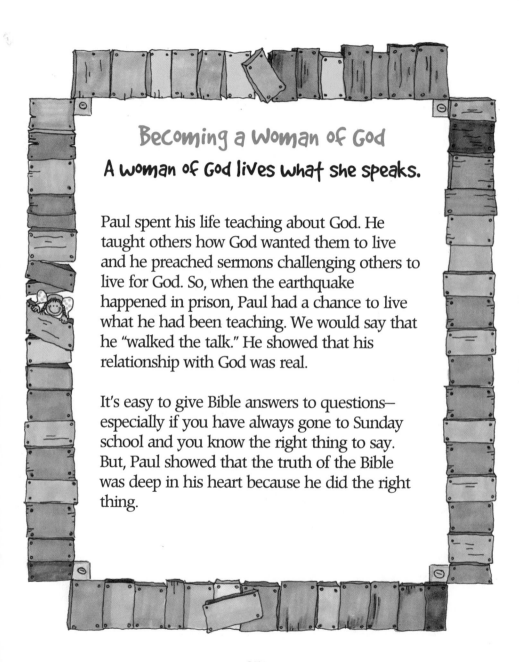

Becoming a Woman of God

A woman of God lives what she speaks.

Paul spent his life teaching about God. He taught others how God wanted them to live and he preached sermons challenging others to live for God. So, when the earthquake happened in prison, Paul had a chance to live what he had been teaching. We would say that he "walked the talk." He showed that his relationship with God was real.

It's easy to give Bible answers to questions—especially if you have always gone to Sunday school and you know the right thing to say. But, Paul showed that the truth of the Bible was deep in his heart because he did the right thing.

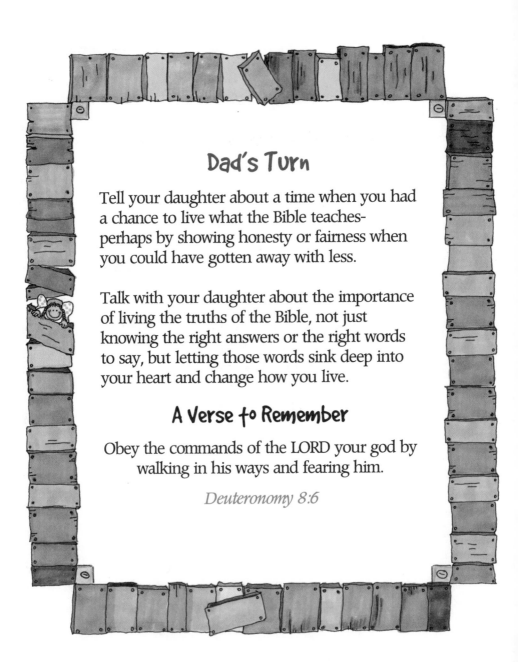

Dad's Turn

Tell your daughter about a time when you had a chance to live what the Bible teaches-perhaps by showing honesty or fairness when you could have gotten away with less.

Talk with your daughter about the importance of living the truths of the Bible, not just knowing the right answers or the right words to say, but letting those words sink deep into your heart and change how you live.

A Verse to Remember

Obey the commands of the LORD your god by walking in his ways and fearing him.

Deuteronomy 8:6

"Uncle Paul, I'm scared. Why did those men put you in prison?" Paul's young nephew visited him at the jail every day.

"They're angry because I teach about God," Paul answered. That confused the boy even more-the men who put him in prison were teachers in the temple. Why should they be angry that Paul taught about God? "It will be OK. Go on home and get some rest," Paul encouraged his young nephew.

In their regular farewell ritual, the boy stuck his hand between the prison bars. Paul grasped the small hand between his own hands for just a second. Then the boy started home. As he rounded a corner he could hear men's voices coming through an open window. They sounded angry. He quietly slipped against the wall and listened for a few minutes. He couldn't believe what he heard!

Racing back to the prison, he called, as loudly as he dared, "Uncle Paul, Uncle Paul! Some men are going to hurt you. They're going to trick the commander into bringing you to the High Council for questioning. Only, they're going to kidnap you and kill you!

"Shhhh, keep your voice down," Paul cautioned. "Are you sure about this?" he whispered.

When the young boy nodded his head, Paul continued, "OK, here's what you've got to do. I'll call the main officer over here and you tell him what you just told me. You are sure, aren't you?"

"Yeah, the men even promised each other that they wouldn't eat anything until you're dead!" the boy's eyes were as big as saucers. He was worried about his uncle's safety.

The brave young man did exactly what Paul told him to do. Quickly the officer arranged for 200 soldiers, 200 spearmen and 70 horsemen to get Paul safely out of town. Paul gave his nephew a big hug before leaving. "You saved my life. I don't know when I'll see you again, but I'll never forget this," he told the boy.

Based on Acts 23:12-35

Becoming a Woman of God
A woman of God tells an adult.

Paul's nephew saved Paul's life. When he heard the bad thing that the men were planning, he told Paul about it. That took courage, didn't it? Paul knew exactly what to do.

Sometimes we may know when there is a problem, but we don't know what to do about it. It's a good idea to tell someone you can trust who is older and wiser.

Have you ever told an adult about some problem you have or that you have heard about? How did it work out? How did the adult help you?

Dad's Turn

If you have a story about confiding in an adult or seeking an adult's help when you were a child, share that story with your daughter. Perhaps there was a time when you should have sought an adult's help and you didn't. Tell her how that situation turned out.

If your daughter has ever confided a problem to you, compliment her on remembering to do that. Talk with her about what kinds of things she might want to talk to an adult about. Help her think of other adults she can trust.

A Verse to Remember

Teach your children to choose the right path, and when they are older, they will remain upon it.

Proverbs 22:6